barbecued!

barbecued!

peter howard

photography by joe filshie

KEY PORTER BOOKS

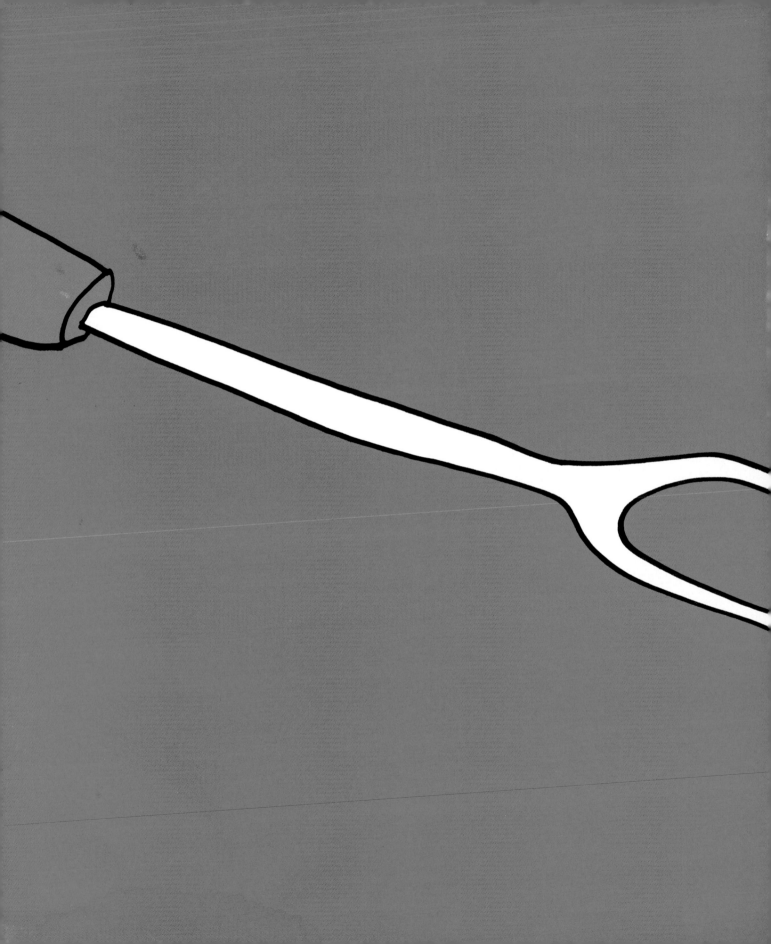

contents

To Grahame Latham A.M.
mentor and mate

Being an end user of great produce for many years now, I am constantly amazed at the quality of fruit, vegetables, meats and so on that I use. Wherever I can, I thank the primary producers of Australia for their dedication and vigilance in keeping these superb products coming to us cooks.

Chef Garry Flynn and a good friend of mine, Brenda Oakley, worked with me on this book to bring it together with passion and speed. Publisher Averill Chase has helped me to find the best way to produce the book and she, and her team, have delivered a book that makes me very proud.

Lastly, to all barbecuers around the world, thanks for the many barbecues I have enjoyed and for inspiring me to write this book.

introduction

Cooking outdoors is common practice in many parts of the world, and barbecuing in particular complements a relaxed and casual lifestyle. My earliest memories of barbecuing involve my father. Not only did he teach me some of the techniques of successful barbecuing, he also introduced me to the social aspects—and that's what has always appealed to me most about barbecuing: folk gathered around with a drink in hand, talking, laughing and enjoying themselves while the food sizzles over smouldering logs. It's a really social experience.

Some of the recipes in this book hark back to those happy days when Dad shared his secrets with me—his delicious onions (we would probably call them caramelised onions today) were cooked slowly and drizzled with a little beer from time to time. Wonderful!

As the barbecue is such a popular method of cooking, we assume that the art comes naturally. Sadly, that's far from the truth. No doubt we've all been to a barbecue where the food was cremated rather than cooked. Skill is definitely involved in good barbecuing but, happily, it can be learned, developed and refined. Take heart—there's a good barbecuer in every one of us.

In this book I offer inspirational advice to empower you to achieve this goal. There are also some taste sensations that even the most hardened 'sausage-and-onion' cook will find hard to resist and success is assured because these recipes have been tried and tested.

Although barbecues themselves come in all shapes and sizes, I choose to use a gas one these days that has a char-grill (with open slats) and a flat plate, allowing me to cook dishes that look great and taste fabulous. They are also less fatty than more traditional barbecue cooking can sometimes be. The recipes in this book have been created for minimum fuss and maximum effect, for the enjoyment of you and your family and friends. Enjoy!

Peter Howard

laws of the barbecue

Always start with a clean barbecue plate.
After you finish cooking, clean it ready for next time. ①

Heat your barbecue to the required temperature well before use. (The temperature is given at the start of each recipe.) ②

Use spray olive oil as opposed to brushing with liquid oil as you have better control over where the oil goes. Although it is not listed in the ingredients for each recipe, you should always have spray olive oil on hand. ③

Always practice good hygiene: don't leave raw ingredients sitting in the sunshine; never let raw meat come into contact with cooked meat and never use leftover marinade as a sauce without cooking it first. ④

Don't mask the natural flavours of your ingredients with too many additions—let their flavours shine through. ⑤

Concentrate on your cooking so that you never end
up with a cremated mess. Use the recipes as a guide
and alter the ingredients to suit your personal taste.

Have the appropriate tools on hand—
tongs or whatever implements suit your needs.

Ensure that the gas tank is filled—this saves you
from the ultimate embarrassment of running out
of 'puff' before the meal is cooked.

As the barbecue is a centre for family entertainment,
be aware of any children around when you are cooking.

The last law always is to enjoy yourself.
A barbecue seems to attract good humour and great
friends so with careful preparation there is nothing
left for you to do but cook and enjoy.

sizzling
starters

chicken koftas

500g (1lb) **chicken**, finely minced
1 medium **onion**, finely chopped
1 medium **green chilli**, seeded and chopped
¼ cup fresh **mint**, chopped
½ teaspoon **salt**
1 teaspoon **garam masala**
½ teaspoon **ground coriander**
½ teaspoon **ground cumin**
½ cup (60g/2oz) dried **breadcrumbs**
bamboo skewers, soaked in water
for 30 minutes before using
mint sprigs, for garnish

These are a variation on a lovely Indian beef dish.
They are moulded onto bamboo skewers—each
skewer is rotated individually for easier cooking.

serves four / high heat / flat plate

in the Kitchen
Combine chicken with onion, chilli, mint, salt, garam masala, coriander, cumin and
breadcrumbs. Knead mixture until stiff and smooth and shape into a small sausage
around one end of each bamboo skewer. (The meat mixture should be about
2.5cm (1in) in diameter and 7.5cm (3in) long.) Lay the koftas on a plate lined
with plastic wrap, cover and refrigerate for one hour.

at the Barbecue
Spray the koftas with oil and cook on the flat plate for nine minutes, turning every minute.

at the Table
Arrange on a platter and decorate with mint sprigs.

6 medium-size **calamari** (squid) tubes, cleaned

coriander (cilantro) sprigs, washed and crisped in the refrigerator, for garnish

FOR THE MARINADE

¼ cup (60ml/2fl oz) **lime juice**

1 tablespoon **peanut oil**

1 small **red chilli**, seeded and minced

1 **coriander root**, washed and minced

1 tablespoon **nam pla** (fish sauce)

2 teaspoons **palm sugar** (jaggery) or dark brown sugar

calamari with lime juice and coriander

I first started cooking calamari in my restaurant in Rockhampton in the mid '70s. I would stuff the tubes with fish mince and braise them in red wine and fish stock until cooked. In those days this was considered an exotic dish, but now calamari is very accessible. It adapts beautifully to the barbecue.

serves four / high heat / open grill

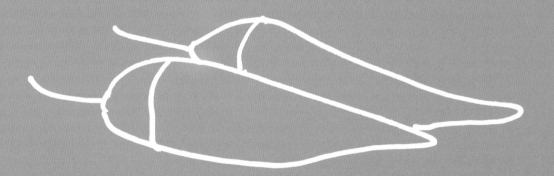

in the Kitchen

Slit each calamari tube down one side and open flat. Score diagonally on the flesh side and cut into bite-size pieces.

Combine marinade ingredients, pour over the scored calamari and marinate for 15 minutes.

at the Barbecue

Lift calamari from marinade and drain off any excess. Spray barbecue with oil and cook calamari on the open grill, in four batches, lifting and tumbling each batch for no longer than four minutes.

at the Table

Lift the pieces onto a warm serving plate and garnish with coriander leaves, torn into smaller pieces to release their aroma. Provide cocktail forks, or napkins if people wish to use their fingers.

½ cup (100g/3½ oz) **couscous**

500g (1lb) lean **minced beef**

60g (2oz) **salad onions** (scallion), chopped

1 teaspoon prepared **curry powder**

1 teaspoon chopped **oregano**

1 **egg**

1 cup (250ml/8fl oz) home-made **barbecue sauce** (see recipe, page 133), to serve

meatballs

with home-made barbecue sauce

When we were kids, Mum used to serve meatballs sitting on spaghetti. I still remember how succulent they were, especially when coated with the homemade tomato sauce she used. This is a variation on her meatballs.

makes 20–24 / medium heat / flat plate

chef's note:
To make it easy to roll the meatballs, wet your hands under running cold water before starting the rolling process.

in the Kitchen

Pour ½ cup boiling water over the couscous in a bowl, cover and leave for three minutes. Fluff with a fork.

Add all the remaining ingredients, except the sauce, and mix well using your hands.

Roll into balls 2.5cm (1in) in diameter (about 25g/1oz each) and place on a plate lined with plastic wrap, cover and refrigerate for two hours.

at the Barbecue

Spray the flat plate with oil and cook meatballs, turning every minute, for six minutes.

at the Table

Place meatballs on a warm platter and serve with the sauce to one side. Leftover sauce will keep, refrigerated, for two weeks.

tiny arancini

440g (14oz) basic **risotto** (see recipe, page 110)
salami, of your choice, cut into 16 x 1cm ($\frac{1}{2}$in) cubes
dry **breadcrumbs**, for coating

I first had arancini at a festival in Griffith, a beautiful thriving, multicultural town in New South Wales, seven hours' drive from Sydney. This flavoursome rice-based ball, about the size of a tennis ball, was stuffed with cheese. It was fabulous but very hard to eat hot as the cheese (mozzarella) was stringy. Here are some tiny versions of that taste sensation, minus the cheese.

serves four / medium heat / flat plate

chef's note:
The arancini may not look cooked on the side but that is alright as the risotto is already fully cooked. I have removed the cheese to eliminate the stringy effect but there is no loss of flavour.

in the Kitchen
Divide cold risotto into 16 equal portions. Push a cube of salami into the middle of each portion and roll/shape into a ball.

Flatten into a round about 4cm (1$\frac{1}{2}$in) in diameter and 2cm ($\frac{3}{4}$in) thick. When you have finished the 16 portions, roll in breadcrumbs, making sure that all excess breadcrumbs are shaken off.

at the Barbecue
Spray flat plate liberally with oil and cook arancini for two minutes. Spray the plate again with oil, turn arancini and cook for another two minutes on the other flat side.

at the Table
Lift arancini onto a serving plate and leave for two minutes before serving.

16 **oysters**, not on shell
16 pieces of rindless **bacon**, each 2.5 x 7.5cm (1 x 3in)
toothpicks
Worcestershire sauce

angels on horseback

These lovely old starters can also have a 'dark side'—devilishly delicious Devils on Horseback, made using pitted prunes instead of oysters. Both variations are scrumptious.

serves four / high heat / flat plate

in the Kitchen
Wrap each oyster in a piece of bacon and secure with a toothpick.

at the Barbecue
Spray flat plate with a little oil. Cook the 'angels' on high heat, brushing with a little Worcestershire sauce as they cook and turning every 30 seconds for two to three minutes, or until oysters are firm and bacon is crisp.

at the Table
Serve the angels on a suitable plate with a little Worcestershire sauce on the side.

scallops with anchovy sauce

To retain their sensual succulence, scallops must be cooked very quickly on a barbecue because they toughen and dry out if overcooked.

serves four / high heat / flat plate

16 **scallops**, with roe
FOR THE ANCHOVY SAUCE
¼ cup (60ml / 2fl oz) **mayonnaise**
1 tablespoon freshly squeezed **lemon juice**
1 tablespoon cold **water**
4 **anchovy** fillets, mashed
4 small sprigs **dill**

in the Kitchen

Remove the black membrane from the side of each scallop.

To make the anchovy sauce, combine all the ingredients and process to a smooth consistency.

at the Barbecue

Spray flat plate with oil and cook scallops for one minute. Turn and cook for one-and-a-half minutes more.

at the Table

Spoon a small amount of sauce into the base of 16 Chinese spoons or dessert spoons. Place a scallop on top of each spoon and drizzle with a little more sauce. Serve on a platter, with the leftover sauce, with the spoon handles pointing outwards.

16 slices **white bread**, crusts removed,
about 10cm (4in) square
butter, at room temperature
English mustard, prepared
16 fresh **asparagus** spears,
about 15cm (6in) long, blanched
16 **toothpicks**

asparagus rolls

The difference between tinned and fresh asparagus is remarkable, but many a cocktail party of the '50s and '60s featured 'savouries' made by wrapping tinned asparagus spears in bread blankets. This is my version of that canapé.

serves four / medium heat / open grill

in the Kitchen

Place a piece of bread on a board and roll it flat with a rolling pin. Smear with a little butter and spread a tiny amount of mustard over the butter.
  Place an asparagus spear diagonally on the buttered bread about 2.5cm (1in) in from one corner and roll from corner to corner. Secure with a toothpick. Repeat with remaining bread and asparagus spears.

at the Barbecue

Spray the rolls with oil and cook on the open grill for four minutes, turning regularly. Lift onto a warm platter.

at the Table

Pass these around, hot off the barbecue.

baba ghanoush

4 **eggplants**, each about 345g (11oz)
4 cloves **garlic**, crushed
1 teaspoon **salt**
½ cup (125ml/4fl oz) **tahini**
¼ cup (60ml/2fl oz) freshly squeezed **lemon juice**
pitta bread or pide (Turkish flat bread)

I remember having this with a mezze plate in a small, fascinating restaurant in Melbourne, Australia. Simplicity is one of the great attractions of this recipe, which gives you a paste that can be used in many ways.

makes about 3 cups (750ml/24fl oz) / medium heat / open grill

in the [K]itchen

Cut eggplants in half lengthwise and score with diagonal cuts to make diamond shapes, being careful not to cut through the skins.

at the [B]arbecue

Spray cut sides of eggplants with oil and cook on the open grill, turning every five minutes, for 35 minutes, or until flesh is soft and skin is charred.

Remove eggplants from the barbecue and cool for 10 minutes before peeling away the skin. You should have about 600g (1lb 4oz) cooked flesh.

Return to the kitchen and blend cooked eggplant, garlic, salt, tahini and lemon juice to a smooth paste.

at the [T]able

Barbecue slices of pitta bread or pide and serve warm with creamy baba ghanoush at room temperature.

tiny sausages
with red capsicum sauce

For all the years I was involved in catering and for all the different cocktail food I have prepared—I wouldn't have any idea how much—chipolatas were always a favourite. Served with this simple dipping sauce, they will get your barbecue off to a really good start.

serves four / high heat / open grill

16 tiny **sausages**/chipolatas
150ml (5fl oz)
red capsicum (bell pepper) **sauce**
(see recipe page 138), to serve

in the [K]itchen
Separate the sausages.

at the [B]arbecue
Cook the tiny sausages on the open grill, turning every minute, for three to four minutes.
  Lift onto paper towels and drain for one minute before serving.

at the [T]able
Serve the sausages on a warm platter with a bowl of the sauce.

from ocean to grill

12 medium-size **raw tiger prawns**,
peeled and deveined with tails left on
2 tablespoons **chilli jam**
(see recipe page 131), to serve

butterflied prawns

served with chilli jam

Only buy your prawns on the day you plan
to cook them. You will know they are cooked
through when they turn opaque.

serves four / high heat / flat plate

chef's note:

Taste the chilli jam before you decide
how much to put on each plate.
If it is 'powerful' use only a little,
as guests can always help themselves
to more if they wish.

in the Kitchen
Butterfly the prawns by slicing down the back of each prawn
from the head end to the tail. (Leave the tails on the prawns
as it helps to hold them together.) Make sure you don't cut right
through to the stomach. Open out the prawn, so that it resembles
a butterfly, and flatten the flesh gently. Take care as the flesh
is very delicate.

at the Barbecue
Spray prawns with oil and cook on the flat plate for 30 seconds.
Turn and cook for 30 seconds longer.

at the Table
Warm the chilli jam and spoon some into the centre of each plate.
Place three cooked prawns on each plate.

4 pieces of **salmon** fillet,
each about 155g (5oz) and about
4cm (1½ in) thick, skin on

FOR THE LEMON MYRTLE RUB

1 teaspoon **ground lemon myrtle**

½ teaspoon **ground pepperberry**

½ teaspoon **ground coriander**

½ teaspoon **ground paprika**

FOR THE CUCUMBER SALAD

220g (7oz) **cucumber**

1 tablespoon **vinegar**

30g (1oz) **sugar**

1 teaspoon **salt**

2 tablespoons finely chopped **dill**

salmon

with lemon myrtle rub and cucumber salad

Not so long ago salmon was considered a great luxury, but thanks to modern farming methods it is now affordable and readily available — a real bonus for barbecuers, because the oil-rich flesh makes salmon ideal for this type of fast, hot cooking.

serves four / medium heat—flat plate / high heat—open grill

in the Kitchen
Mix the lemon myrtle rub ingredients together, then sprinkle and massage the rub into the flesh side of the salmon. You can use a liberal amount of the rub as the salmon's big flavour can cope with the rub's complexity.

For the cucumber salad, peel cucumber, scoop out seeds with a teaspoon and slice flesh into half-moons. Combine with remaining ingredients, stir well, cover and refrigerate.

at the Barbecue
Spray the flat plate with oil and cook fish, flesh-side-down, for two minutes.

Spray skin side of salmon and lift carefully onto the open grill, skin-side-down. Cook for a further minute, or until the skin is crisp but not burned.

Turn and stand each fish piece on its side and cook for one minute. Repeat this on the other side for one minute. (If you prefer your fish cooked more than I have suggested, by all means do so.)

at the Table
Serve fish on individual plates with cucumber salad on the side. A lively green salad is ideal to serve with this dish.

For people who don't like the crisp fish skin, the flesh will slip easily from the skin once it is cooked.

barbecued gravlax of ocean trout
with barbecued potatoes

Ocean trout have a marvellous flesh structure and brilliant flavour that lends itself very well to the Scandinavian preserving treatment. This recipe takes the process just one step further.

serves four / medium heat—flat plate / medium heat—open grill

4 pieces of **ocean trout** fillet, each about 155g (5oz), skin on
5 tablespoons freshly chopped **dill**
60g (2oz) **demerara sugar**
30g (1oz) **sea salt**
FOR THE BARBECUED POTATOES
8 medium **waxy potatoes**, cut in half lengthwise and par-boiled for 5 minutes
½ teaspoon **sea salt**

in the Kitchen

Place two pieces of trout, skin-side-down, in a container lined with plastic wrap. Combine dill, sugar and salt and mix well. Sprinkle the dill mixture over the fish in the container.

Put remaining two pieces of fish, flesh-side-down, on top of the dill. Cover with plastic wrap, pressing it closely over the fish, and put weights on top. Leave in the refrigerator for 24 hours.

at the Barbecue

Spray the flat plate liberally with oil. Shake excess dill mixture from the fish and cook, flesh-side-down, for two minutes. Spray the skin with oil and turn. Cook on the second side for a further three minutes, or until done to your liking.

Turn and stand each fish piece on its side and cook for one minute. Repeat this on the other side for one minute.

Spray cut side of potatoes with oil and cook, cut-side-down, on the open grill for two minutes. Sprinkle with salt and cook for a further two minutes, or until cooked through.

at the Table

Spoon some barbecued potatoes on one side of each plate and serve a piece of trout, skin-side-down, resting against them.

lobster

2 **raw lobster tails**, each 345g (11oz),
thawed and cut in half lengthwise

155g (5oz) **unsalted butter**, melted

juice of 1 **lime**

2cm (¾in) **lemongrass**, white part only, finely chopped

½ teaspoon **pink peppercorns**, crushed

¼ teaspoon **sea salt**

in the shell with lemongrass and lime flavours

You can buy frozen raw lobster tails from good fishmongers but you may have to order them in advance because they're not an everyday item.

serves four / medium heat—flat plate / medium heat—open grill

in the Kitchen

Retaining the shells, gently lift the flesh from the lobster tails and cut into bite-size pieces. Put the tail meat, melted butter, lime juice, lemongrass, peppercorns and salt in a bowl and tumble.

Pack the meat back into the half-shells and press down firmly. Place on a plate, cover and refrigerate for one hour. The butter will set the meat in place. Reserve any butter and lobster juices that may be left in the bowl.

at the Barbecue

Place half-shells, flesh-side-down, on the flat plate—use your hand to hold the meat in place as you slide it onto the barbecue. Cook for two minutes.

Very carefully slide a long spatula underneath each cooking half-shell and lift it, turning it flesh-side-up, onto the open grill.

Cook for five minutes and drizzle any reserved butter and lobster juices into the half-shells. To get the half-shells to sit up, rest them against each other. This is important so that the juices don't leak out.

at the Table

Serve half-shells on a platter with crisp, dressed salad leaves.

barbecued tuna steak 'niçoise'

This particular style of serving tuna attracts plenty of attention—especially as there are those who think you should only use canned tuna. Certainly, that is the way I first saw it served. But, after I enjoyed chef Iain Hewitson's variation using fresh tuna, in Melbourne some years ago, I was sold on this style of Niçoise.

serves four / high heat / flat plate

¼ cup (60ml/2fl oz) extra virgin **olive oil**

30ml (1fl oz) **wine vinegar**

155g (5oz) **green beans**, whole, topped, tailed and blanched

155g (5oz) **Desirée potatoes**, sliced 2cm (¾in) thick and par-boiled for 5 minutes

4 x 125g (4oz) **tuna steaks**, about 2cm (¾in) thick

3 **Roma** (plum) **tomatoes**, trimmed at either end and cut into wedges

2 hard-boiled **eggs**, peeled and quartered

20 black **olives**

4–8 **anchovy** fillets

cracked **black pepper** (optional)

in the Kitchen

Mix olive oil and vinegar together.

at the Barbecue

Lightly spray beans with oil and toss on the flat plate. Move these around quickly for one minute and don't let them brown. Lift onto a platter.

Spray potato slices with oil and cook on each side for one minute, or until done. Lift and place on the beans.

Spray tuna with oil and cook on the flat plate for one minute on each side.

Meanwhile, spread tomatoes, hard-boiled eggs and black olives over the top of the potatoes and beans. Arrange anchovy fillets on the vegetables. Remove tuna from barbecue and arrange on top.

at the Table

Spoon oil and vinegar dressing over the tuna and sprinkle with cracked black pepper, if desired.

500g (1lb) **waxy potatoes**, peeled and chopped
250g (8oz) **canned red salmon**, drained
1 tablespoon **capers**, chopped
1 large **egg**, beaten lightly
2 tablespoons **dried breadcrumbs**
1 teaspoon **salt**
good pinch of **cayenne pepper**
soft breadcrumbs, for coating
lemon and mustard butter (see recipe page 134), to serve

barbecued salmon cakes

Mashed potato is used in this dish to extend the salmon, a throwback to former times when canned salmon was more of a luxury. Even though we now see plenty of fresh salmon, these salmon patties or cakes remain a favourite.

serves four / medium heat / flat plate

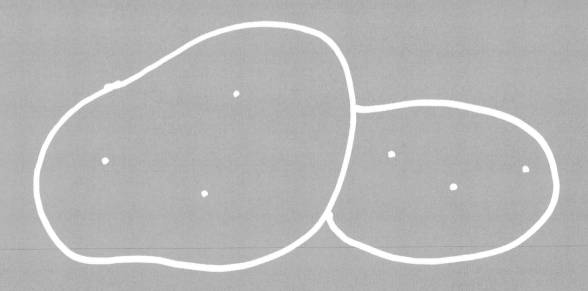

in the Ⓚitchen

Cover potatoes with water and bring to the boil. Reduce to a simmer and cook until tender. Drain well, tip into a mixing bowl and mash until smooth. Set aside to cool. (If the potatoes are too wet, your salmon-cake mixture will be too soft and hard to shape.)

When cool, add salmon, capers and egg to potato and, using your hands, mix well. The salmon should be evenly distributed through the potato with no lumps of salmon visible. Mix in half the dried breadcrumbs. You may not need all the breadcrumbs—it depends on how moist the mixture is. The mixture is ready for use when it comes away easily from your fingertips.

Roll and shape the mixture into eight patties, about 6cm (2½in) in diameter and 2cm (¾in) thick. Place on a plate covered in plastic wrap, cover with more plastic wrap and refrigerate for at least two hours before use.

Roll the patties in soft breadcrumbs to coat lightly.

at the Ⓑarbecue

Spray the flat plate liberally with oil and cook patties for three minutes on one side. Turn them over and cook for a further two minutes on the other side.

at the Ⓣable

Serve salmon cakes on individual plates with lemon and mustard butter and steamed vegetables.

chef's note:

When adding dry ingredients to wet in cooking, as when adding the dry breadcrumbs to the potato mixture in this recipe, the general rule is not to add them all at once. It's easy to add a little more, but you can never take them out if you've added too much.

24 Pacific **oysters**, freshly shucked, on the shell

24 tiny sprigs of **dill**

⅓ cup (80ml/3fl oz) Stolichnaya **vodka**

6 tablespoons **salmon or lumpfish roe**

drunken oysters

A surefire way to get your party going is to serve oysters this way. They're ready in a jiffy and look spectacular. Pass them around with napkins and watch your guests slip the oysters into their mouths in a slightly decadent way that really suits the outdoor scene.

serves four / high heat / open grill

in the Kitchen
Rinse oysters under slow-flowing water to remove all shell fragments. Wash dill and crisp in the refrigerator. Pour vodka into a small jug.

at the Barbecue
Cook oysters in their shells on the open grill for two minutes. During cooking, splash a little vodka on the oysters with a spoon. Do not pour from the bottle or jug in case the alcohol catches fire.

at the Table
Carefully lift oysters onto a platter or onto individual plates. Top with ½ teaspoon of salmon roe and a sprig of dill.

500g (1lb) **white fish**, such as snapper

2 tablespoons finely chopped **chives**

2 **egg whites**, beaten lightly

1 clove **garlic**, finely chopped

4 **candlenuts**, or blanched almonds, chopped roughly

¼ teaspoon freshly grated **nutmeg**

½ teaspoon dried **shrimp paste**

1 fresh **Kaffir lime leaf**, vein removed and leaf shredded

1 tablespoon **nam pla** (fish sauce)

1 tablespoon finely chopped **lemongrass**

lime wedges, to serve

fish patties with Indonesian flavours

Nothing has been imitated as often as Thai fish cakes but this is an Indonesian version that I fell in love with when I was in Bali.

serves four / medium heat / flat plate

in the Kitchen

Bone fish and chop finely by pulsing in a food processor, or putting through a mincer.
(However you do it, the mince must be fine.)

Combine all ingredients, except lime wedges, and, using your hands, mix well.
Cover and refrigerate overnight.

Dip your hands in cold water and leave them wet to shape the fish patties to the size you desire.
Mine are 5cm (2in) in diameter and 1cm (½in) thick—they work out about 50g (1½oz) each.
Place on a plate lined with plastic wrap, cover with more plastic wrap and refrigerate for one hour.

at the Barbecue

Spray one side of the fish cakes liberally with oil and cook, oiled-side-down, on the flat plate
for two minutes. Spray again with oil, turn them over and cook for a further two minutes.

at the Table

Lift patties onto a serving platter, decorate with lime wedges and serve with steamed or fried rice.

If you like, serve with some light soy sauce flavoured with a little sweet chilli dipping sauce,
but these patties really have plenty of flavour on their own.

8 free-range **eggs**

3 tablespoons chopped **chives**

30g (1oz) **butter**, melted and returned to room temperature

¼ teaspoon freshly ground **black pepper**

4–8 slices **brioche**

8 slices **smoked salmon**

chived eggs with

smoked salmon and brioche

Scrambled eggs and smoked salmon are one of the classic combinations. Chives add a wonderful flavour and the brioche provides a textural component that balances this simple dish.

serves four / medium heat—flat plate / high heat—open grill

in the Kitchen

Take two bowls and beat four eggs well in each bowl. Stir half the chives, butter and black pepper into each batch.

at the Barbecue

Spray brioche lightly with oil and toast on both sides on the open grill. Place slice(s) on four individual plates and start cooking the eggs.

Oil the flat plate liberally and pour one batch of eggs on—use a spatula to keep them from running all over the plate. This is like making eggs in a frying pan rather than a saucepan—you must keep the egg mixture constantly moving around a concentrated area on the barbecue plate. Each batch will take 45 to 50 seconds to cook and must retain a gloss on the top.

Divide the first batch of scrambled eggs between two of the plates, placing on top of the brioche. Cook the second batch in the same way, and divide between the remaining two plates.

at the Table

Top scrambled eggs with the salmon slices and serve immediately.

chef's note:

To cook eggs this way it is essential that your flat plate is very clean.

32 **mussels**

2 small **zucchinis**

4 small **bok choy** (Chinese chard)

8 fresh **asparagus** spears

2 tablespoons **balsamic vinegar**

¼ cup (60ml/2fl oz) extra virgin **olive oil**

½ teaspoon freshly ground **black pepper**

4 **red capsicum** (bell pepper) wedges

mussels

with barbecued summer vegetables

Be sure to buy your mussels only on the day you are going to cook them. When you are preparing the mussels in the kitchen, discard any with broken shells and any open ones that do not shut when firmly tapped. Also discard any cooked ones that do not open.

serves four / high and medium heat / open grill

in the [K]itchen

Soak mussels in cold water for a couple of hours; scrub to remove beards and any extra hairy bits on the shell.

Halve zucchini and bok choy lengthwise. Trim asparagus, leaving no white part. Whisk balsamic vinegar, olive oil and black pepper together.

at the [B]arbecue

Spray zucchini and capsicum with olive oil and cook on the open grill over medium heat for seven to eight minutes, turning regularly until browned.

Add bok choy and asparagus and cook, turning regularly, on the open grill over medium heat for three minutes.

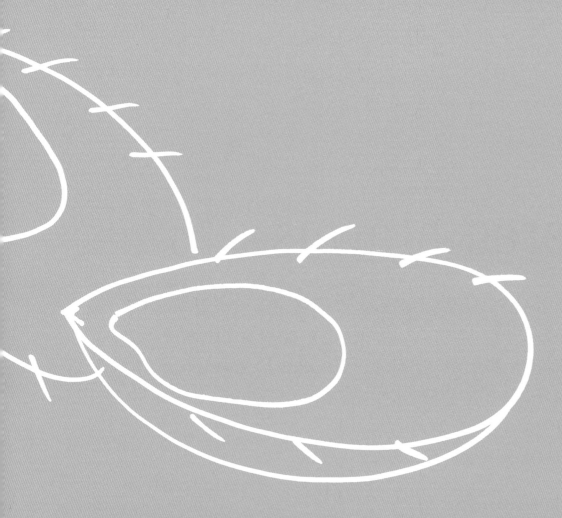

When you start to cook the zucchini and capsicum, place the mussels on the open grill over high heat. As the shells start to open, after one to two minutes, spread them so that they sit as flat as possible on the barbecue, flesh-side-down. They will emit steam, so be careful when lifting them. Leave them to cook for another 30 seconds and lift carefully from the barbecue into a bowl to catch the cooking juices.

When mussels are cool enough to handle, ease the flesh from the shells into the balsamic vinegar mixture along with the cooking juices. Mix well and leave to sit for five minutes.

at the Table

Place half a bok choy in the centre of each plate, top with a capsicum wedge, a zucchini half and two asparagus spears. Sit equal portions of mussels on top and spoon over the balsamic-flavoured juices.

16 medium-size **raw tiger prawns**,
peeled and deveined
bamboo skewers, soaked for 30 minutes in water
light **olive oil**
4 **lemon** wedges

skewered prawns

with barbecued lemon

I first saw barbecued lemons used at a chef's private party and was struck by the marvellous change in the lemon flavour induced by barbecuing. Skewering prawns keeps them straight and helps them to cook evenly.

serves four / medium heat / open grill and flat plate

in the K̲itchen

Insert the skewer into the tail of each prawn and thread the meat on so that the flesh is kept straight.

Arrange the skewered prawns on a flat plate and drizzle with light olive oil. Rotate the prawns to coat them with oil.

at the B̲arbecue

Cook lemon wedges, flesh-side-down, on the open grill for one minute.

Cook prawns on the flat plate for three minutes, turning them constantly and drizzling with the oil they were sitting in.

at the T̲able

Remove skewers and put four prawns on each plate with a barbecued lemon wedge. Serve at once.

24 **oysters**, freshly shucked, on shell
¼ cup (60ml/2fl oz) **garlic oil** (see recipe page 135)
24 thin slices of **preserved lemon** rind, each 2.5cm (1in)
long, washed and flesh discarded
freshly cracked **black pepper**

oysters with preserved lemon and garlic oil

The Moroccans have a marvellous way of preserving lemons. Preserved lemons add another flavour dimension to oysters—but use sparingly as the flavour is intense.

serves four / high heat / open grill

in the Kitchen
Rinse oysters under slow-flowing water to remove all shell fragments.

at the Barbecue
Drizzle oysters in their shells with a little garlic oil and cook flesh-side-up on the open grill for one to two minutes. When the rims of the oysters starts to bubble, they are ready to serve.

at the Table
Place oysters on four individual plates and top each with a slice of preserved lemon. Sprinkle with cracked pepper. Be careful handling the shells—they can be very hot and cooking will continue for a couple of minutes after they are removed from the heat.

whole sardines

with capers and pinenuts

12 fresh **sardines**, cleaned (gut removed)
$\frac{1}{4}$ cup **capers**, drained and washed
45g (1$\frac{1}{2}$oz) **pinenuts**
$\frac{1}{4}$ teaspoon **ground cumin**
lemon wedges, to serve (optional)

This simple dish evokes images of harbourside cooking all along the Mediterranean. Fresh sardines, about 12cm (5in) long, are easily available in supermarkets, and their rich, oily flesh makes them a natural for cooking on the barbecue.

serves four / medium heat / flat plate

in the Kitchen

Rinse sardines and pat dry. Combine capers and pinenuts.

at the Barbecue

Spray the flat plate with oil and cook sardines for one-and-a-half minutes. Spray sardines with oil and, using a long spatula, gently turn them over. Cook for a further one-and-a-half minutes.

Meanwhile, pour the capers and pinenuts onto the flat plate. Cook for three minutes, tossing and moving them about but keeping them in a concentrated area. The pinenuts will be lightly browned and the capers warmed through.

Lift capers and pinenuts from the barbecue, place at one end of a platter and sprinkle with cumin. Remove sardines from the barbecue and place on the same platter.

at the Table

The sardines can be eaten whole, bones and all, with the capers and pinenuts as a tasty addition. Serve with lemon wedges, if desired.

4 x 155g (5oz) **fish** fillets, such as
red snapper, grouper or sea bream
400g (14oz) **potatoes**, peeled and chopped
125g (4oz) **butter**
60g (2oz) brown **shallots**, finely chopped
½ teaspoon **sea salt**
¼ teaspoon **cayenne pepper**
FOR THE DUCK-EGG DILL MAYONNAISE
2 **duck egg yolks**
1 teaspoon prepared **American mustard**
1 tablespoon freshly squeezed **lemon juice**
1 cup (250ml/8fl oz) light **olive oil**,
or vegetable oil
1 tablespoon chopped **dill**
½ teaspoon **salt**

fillet of fish
with mash and duck-egg dill mayonnaise

The firm flesh of fish like red snapper, grouper and sea bream make them naturals for cooking on the barbecue and they have always been favourites of mine. They certainly featured strongly on the menu of my first restaurant in Rockhampton. I also really like duck eggs, which I use not only to make mayonnaise with, but also ice-cream.

serves four / medium heat / flat plate

in the Ⓚitchen

Trim fish, if necessary, and pat dry. Cover potatoes with water and bring to the boil. Reduce to a simmer and cook until tender. Test with a sharp knife to ensure potatoes are cooked through.

Drain and return potatoes to the saucepan. Add butter, shallots, salt and pepper. Leave to sit for three minutes with the lid on, then mash roughly. Spoon into a microwave-proof bowl, cover and keep at room temperature.

To make the mayonnaise, combine egg yolks, mustard and lemon juice in a food processor. Pulse for one minute then, with the machine running, slowly dribble in half the oil. Pour in remainder at a slow, constant speed to form a thick mayonnaise. If the mixture becomes too thick, pour in a tablespoon of warm water and continue to add the oil.

Transfer mayonnaise from the processor to a serving bowl. Sprinkle in dill and salt and stir to combine. This dressing should be the consistency of pouring cream. It can be thinned by adding more lemon juice or water—depending on how much you like the flavour of lemon.

at the Ⓑarbecue

Spray fish with oil and cook on the flat plate for two minutes. Spray again with oil, turn over and cook for a further three minutes, or until done to your liking. The cooking time depends on the thickness of the fish—mine was 3cm (just over 1in) thick. When the juices that come to the top of the fish become milky, the fish is cooked.

While the fish is cooking, reheat the mash, covered, in the microwave on medium for two minutes, stir and microwave for one minute more.

at the Ⓣable

Spoon portions of mash into the centre of individual plates. Lean a piece of fish against the potato and drizzle with 1 tablespoon of the duck-egg dill mayonnaise.

chef's note:
Duck eggs have a much stronger flavour than hen eggs, so this mayonnaise
is anything but bland. Please taste it before serving judiciously. Hen eggs
can be subsituted if duck eggs are unavailable.

lobster medallions

with sichuan peppercorns and orange dressing

You can see that lobster meat is very delicate just by looking at it, so treat it gently. Sichuan peppercorns are sweeter and more fragrant than other types of dried peppercorns and highlight the flavours of the lobster.

serves four / medium heat / flat plate

2 **raw lobster tails**, each 255g (9oz), thawed and cut in half lengthwise

2 tablespoons **Sichuan peppercorns**, crushed with 1 teaspoon **sea salt** in a mortar and pestle

FOR THE ORANGE DRESSING

½ cup (125ml/4fl oz) **vegetable oil**

¼ cup (60ml/2fl oz) freshly squeezed **orange juice**

¼ teaspoon **sea salt**

1 tablespoon finely chopped **Vietnamese mint**

rind of 1 small **orange**, finely grated

in the Kitchen

Gently lift the flesh from the lobster tails and discard shells. Cut flesh into medallions, or 1cm (½in) diagonal slices (you will get about 6 slices per tail). Sprinkle half the peppercorn and salt mixture evenly over one side of the medallions.

To make dressing, combine ingredients and mix well.

at the Barbecue

Spray the flat plate liberally with oil and cook lobster medallions, peppercorn-sprinkled-side-down, for one minute.

Spray with oil, sprinkle with remaining peppercorn mixture and turn. Cook for a further two minutes and lift from the barbecue to a warm serving plate.

at the Table

Spoon the dressing over the lobster and serve with cooked rice noodles and steamed Chinese greens.

chef's note:
If Vietnamese mint is unavailable, substitute regular mint, although the flavour is different.

16 **scallops**, on shell

125g (4oz) **salad onion** (scallion) tops, finely sliced

rind of 1 **lime**, blanched and julienned

FOR THE SAUCE

2 tablespoon **soy sauce**

1 tablespoon **sweet chilli sauce**

1 teaspoon finely chopped **fresh ginger**

1 tablespoon **lime juice**

2 teaspoons **water**

scallops on shell
with asian flavours

These delicate beauties must be protected from fierce heat, and this is done by resting them on a bed of salad onions— a great flavouring ingredient. The scallops are enhanced by the delicious Asian flavours.

serves four / medium heat / open grill

in the Kitchen

Lift each scallop from the shell, remove black membrane and set the flesh to one side. Distribute equal amounts of salad onion tops into each shell and rest the scallop on top.

To make the sauce, combine ingredients and mix well.

at the Barbecue

Place prepared scallops, in their shells, flesh-side-up on the open grill and spoon ½ teaspoon of sauce over each. Cook for three minutes and drizzle each with another ½ teaspoon of sauce. Remove from barbecue.

at the Table

Place four scallop shells on each plate and garnish each with a few strands of lime rind.

4 **snapper**, each 500g (16oz)

1 small **lemon**, cut into quarters

8 **salad onions** (scallion), white parts only

90g (3oz) **butter**, melted

1 teaspoon **sea salt**

$\frac{1}{2}$ teaspoon freshly ground **black pepper**

4 sheets of **aluminium foil**, sprayed with oil

FOR THE LENTIL AND SPANISH ONION SALAD

250g (8oz) **dried green lentils**, washed

2$\frac{1}{2}$ cups (625ml/20fl oz) **water**

1 small **Spanish onion** (red onion), roughly chopped

125g (4oz) **red capsicum** (bell pepper), diced

1 cup **mint** leaves

$\frac{1}{2}$ cup (125ml/4fl oz) **mayonnaise**

$\frac{1}{4}$ cup (60ml/2fl oz) extra virgin **olive oil**

2 tablespoons Spanish **sherry vinegar**

1 teaspoon **salt**

$\frac{1}{2}$ teaspoon **turmeric**

whole snapper
with lentil and spanish onion salad

As I was brought up in the country, we rarely saw ocean fish. For us, freshwater fish such as silver perch and catfish were the order of the day, and every now and then an eel, which none of us would eat. When I discovered snapper I thought it was the most beautiful fish I had ever eaten and it has remained one of my favourites ever since.

serves four / medium heat / flat plate

in the [K]itchen

Rinse fish cavities with cold water and dry with paper towel. Cut two deep diagonal slashes into each side of each fish.

Lay one fish on each piece of oiled foil and stuff each gut cavity with a lemon quarter and two salad onions. (You may have to cut the salad onions to fit in the cavity.) Spoon over the melted butter and sprinkle with salt and pepper.

Wrap fish in the foil, making sure that the foil is tight around the fish so that the juices can't escape during cooking. Refrigerate parcels for 30 minutes.

For the salad, place lentils in a saucepan and add water. Bring to the boil and simmer for 20 to 25 minutes, skimming the top of the water during cooking to remove the brown froth. The lentils should be tender but holding their shape.

Remove from heat, strain and rinse under cold water for 30 seconds. Drain and pour into a salad bowl. Add onion and capsicum. Tear mint leaves into pieces as you add them to the lentils.

Pour in the mayonnaise, oil, sherry vinegar, salt and turmeric. Stir well to combine flavours and set aside to cool to room temperature.

at the [B]arbecue

Place fish parcels on the flat plate and cook for eight minutes on each side.

at the [T]able

Lift fish parcels onto individual plates and allow each person to open the foil to reveal the beautifully cooked fish. The wonderful aroma of lemon and salad onion escapes as the parcels are opened. Serve the lentil salad in the centre of the table with a mixed leaf salad.

chef's note:
If you are lucky enough to find fish with scales intact, please leave them on. The scales help retain the moisture in the fish and you will find that they come away from the flesh very easily with the skin.

4 fresh **rainbow trout**, each 200g (7oz),
gutted and cleaned
1 medium **onion**, sliced into rings
1 cup (250g/8oz) **couscous**
1 tablespoon extra virgin **olive oil**
4 **lemon** wedges
60g (2oz) **dukkah**, ready-made

rainbow trout with dukkah and couscous

There's a wonderful earthiness in the flavour of rainbow trout that I find very attractive. The succulent flesh doesn't need fancy sauces.

serves four / medium heat—open grill / medium heat—flat plate

in the Kitchen

Rinse inside cavities of trout and dry with paper towel; pat the skin dry.

Pour 1 cup boiling water over couscous in a bowl, cover and leave for three minutes. Add oil, fluff with a fork and keep warm.

at the Barbecue

Lightly oil the flat plate and cook onion rings over medium heat until lightly browned. At the same time spray trout and cook on the open grill over medium heat for five minutes on each side.

Remove onions and return to the kitchen to mix them through the couscous. Cover and reheat in the microwave on medium high for two minutes.

at the Table

Serve trout alongside couscous on individual plates. Garnish each with a lemon wedge and serve the dukkah separately. Eat the trout skin along with the cooked fish, sprinkling dukkah over each mouthful.

chef's note:
Dukkah is an Egyptian mixture of crushed hazelnuts, crushed pistachios, sesame seeds, ground coriander, ground cumin, salt and pepper. Look for it in Middle Eastern shops.

chicken, duck and quail

6 **chicken thighs**, boned and trimmed of all fat

½ cup (125ml/4fl oz) freshly squeezed **lime juice**

3 **Kaffir lime leaves**, vein removed, finely shredded

1 tablespoon finely chopped **fresh ginger**

1 large **green chilli**, seeded and chopped

30g (1oz) **white sugar**

1 tablespoon **peanut oil**

1 cup (250ml/8fl oz) **peanut sauce** (see recipe page 137)

8 sprigs fresh **coriander** (cilantro)

lime-marinated
chicken with peanut sauce

Chicken thighs are used in this recipe as they adapt to the marvellous marinade flavours so well. They also retain their moisture when cooked on the barbecue in this fashion.

serves four / medium heat / flat plate

in the Kitchen

Cut chicken thighs in half so you have 12 pieces. Combine the lime juice, lime leaf, ginger, chilli and sugar, stirring well. Pour over the chicken thighs, coating the meat well with the marinade. Cover and refrigerate for 30 minutes.

at the Barbecue

Oil the flat plate with the peanut oil. Remove chicken thighs from the marinade and drain well, reserving marinade. Cook chicken for two minutes on each side, basting with reserved marinade.
  With a sharp knife and a set of tongs, cut the chicken thighs into strips about 1cm (½in) wide (on the flat plate). Move the chicken pieces to a central area and pour over half the peanut sauce. Lift and toss the chicken so the sauce coats the pieces. Cook for a total of nine minutes.

at the Table

Lift the chicken onto a warm platter and pour over the remaining peanut sauce. Garnish with coriander sprigs and serve with boiled rice or boiled vermicelli noodles.

barbecued chicken breast
with parsley salad

There is no doubting the versatility of chicken in all areas of cooking and this recipe is simplicity itself.

serves four / medium heat / flat plate and open grill

4 x 155g (5oz) **chicken breasts**, skin removed

FOR THE PARSLEY SALAD

155g (5oz) **curly parsley**, washed and roughly chopped

10 **basil** leaves

60g (2oz) **peanuts**, roasted and crushed

1 large **green capsicum** (bell pepper), halved, seeded and roughly chopped

2 **salad onions** (scallion), roughly chopped

30g (1oz) **demerara sugar**

2 tablespoons **nam pla** (fish sauce)

2 tablespoons **peanut oil**

1 tablespoon **rice vinegar**

in the Kitchen

Butterfly the chicken breasts by slicing through the thick part of each breast, taking care not to slice through completely. Open out so that you have a butterfly shaped piece of meat.

Make the salad by combining parsley, basil, peanuts, capsicum and salad onions. Combine sugar, fish sauce, oil and vinegar and mix well until sugar is dissolved. Add dressing to the salad and toss well. Cover and refrigerate.

at the Barbecue

Spray the cut side of the chicken and cook on the flat plate for one minute. Spray the uncut side with oil, flip the chicken breast over and cook the second side for another minute.

Lift the chicken breast onto the open grill and cook for a further one-and-a-half minutes on each side. Remove the chicken breast, drain on paper towel and return to the kitchen. Cut chicken breasts into halves along the existing cut lines so that you have eight pieces of chicken of similar size.

at the Table

Place two pieces of chicken on the centre of each plate to form a 'V'. Spoon some parsley salad into the 'V' and serve.

chicken livers

12 medium-size **chicken livers**,
about 440g (14oz) altogether
4 bamboo or metal **skewers** (soak bamboo
skewers in water for 30 minutes before using)
90g (3oz) dried **breadcrumbs**
1 tablespoon ground **dried marjoram**
1 tablespoon freshly squeezed **lemon juice**
1 teaspoon finely chopped **fresh marjoram**
2 teaspoons **olive oil**

with lemon and marjoram baste

Years ago I lived in Adelaide, where I had some lovely
Greek friends. This was one of the many delightful dishes
served at their home.

serves four / medium heat / flat plate

in the Kitchen
Trim chicken livers to remove all cores and fat and slide three livers onto each skewer.
Combine breadcrumbs and dried marjoram and roll the chicken livers in the breadcrumb
mixture. Combine lemon juice, fresh marjoram and olive oil.

at the Barbecue
Spray the flat plate liberally with oil and cook crumbed chicken livers for one minute. Spray chicken
livers with oil again, turn and cook for a further minute on the other side. You will have to use a
spatula to ease the livers from the plate. Repeat this cooking once, so that the chicken livers have
finally been cooked for two minutes on each side for medium-cooked livers. If you want them well-
done, cook them a little longer. In the last minute of cooking, spoon over a little of the lemon juice
mixture. Lift from the barbecue onto a platter. Rest for two minutes before serving.

at the Table
Spoon remaining lemon juice mixture over the chicken livers and serve with steamed rice.

500g (1lb) **chicken breast** meat

1 tablespoon **corn oil**

1 tablespoon Spanish **sherry vinegar**

1 tablespoon **ground allspice**

2 teaspoons **dried oregano**

2 tablespoons **onion flakes**

1 teaspoon **salt**

¼ teaspoon **chilli powder** (optional)

8 wheat flour **tortillas**

2 cups shredded **lettuce**

1 cup shaved **carrot**

2 medium-size salad **tomatoes**, cut into wedges

½ cup (125ml/4fl oz) **sour cream**

chicken fajitas

I was introduced to lamb fajitas in Chicago, at the National Restaurant Association Show—I cooked Australian lamb and beef there for five years. Here, I have adapted those ideas to chicken.

serves four / high heat / flat plate and open grill

in the Kitchen

Cut chicken breast across the grain into strips 1cm (½in) wide and place in a bowl.

Combine the oil, sherry vinegar, allspice, oregano, onion flakes, salt and chilli powder, if using. Pour marinade over the chicken, stirring to coat the pieces thoroughly. Cover and refrigerate for at least two hours.

at the Barbecue

Spray the flat plate with oil and tip on the chicken strips—spread over the plate and cook by tossing and lifting the pieces, allowing them to brown. The chicken meat should cook in six minutes.

Spray tortillas with oil and cook on the open grill for 30 seconds on each side. When tortillas are warm, remove from the open grill, lift the chicken onto a platter and return to the kitchen. Heap lettuce, carrot and tomatoes around the chicken.

at the Table

Serve the chicken platter, tortillas and sour cream and let everybody assemble their own fajitas.

4 x 155g (5oz) **chicken breast**, skin on
2 tablespoons extra virgin **olive oil**

FOR THE TZATZIKI

1 **cucumber**, about 25cm (10in) long
1 teaspoon **salt**
2 cloves **garlic**, peeled and crushed
1½ cups (375ml/12fl oz) plain thick **yoghurt**
1 tablespoon dried **mint**
1 tablespoon extra virgin **olive oil**

FOR THE GREEK SALAD

1 medium-size head **iceberg lettuce**,
washed and crisped
2 medium-size **tomatoes**, cut into wedges
125g (4oz) **feta cheese**, diced
20 Kalamata **olives**
2 tablespoons **lemon juice**
1 tablespoon extra virgin **olive oil**

chicken breast

with tzatziki and greek salad

Greeks have left their mark on cooking all around the world. There are versions of moussaka no matter where you go in the Western world. The chicken breast in Greece would more than likely be cooked over smouldering coals, but this is my version done on a regular barbecue.

serves four / medium heat / flat plate and open grill

in the Kitchen

Trim the chicken breast and soak in olive oil.

To make the tzatziki, cut the cucumber in half lengthwise. Using a teaspoon, scoop out and discard seeds. Peel each half and slice into very fine half-moon shapes. Place in a bowl, sprinkle with salt and tumble. Leave to sit for one hour.

Rinse cucumber under cold water to remove salt and tip onto paper towels to drain. Pat the cucumber as dry as possible and place in a serving bowl. Add garlic, yoghurt, mint and olive oil and stir well. Refrigerate for at least one hour before serving.

For the salad, break the crisped lettuce into bite-size pieces in a salad bowl. Add tomatoes and tumble in the cheese and olives. Cover and refrigerate. Leave the lemon juice and olive oil to one side.

at the Barbecue

Place chicken, skin-side-down, on the flat plate and cook for two minutes. Drizzle chicken with a little of the oil it was soaking in, turn over and cook for a further two minutes.

Lift chicken breast onto the open grill and cook for two minutes on the skin side. Turn over and cook for a further two minutes.

Remove the chicken from the barbecue onto paper towel, return to the kitchen and leave in a warm place to rest for four minutes before serving.

at the Table

Spoon some tzatziki on one side of each plate. Slice the chicken across the grain into rounds and arrange in a fan around the tzatziki. Drizzle combined lemon juice and olive oil over the salad and toss well.

4 x 155g (5oz) Muscovy **duck breasts**

4 medium-size **bok choy** (Chinese chard)

220g (7oz) **celeriac**

1 tablespoon **white vinegar**

2 medium **shallots**, peeled and finely diced

½ cup (125ml/4fl oz) basic handmade **mayonnaise**
(see recipe page 129)

1 tablespoon Japanese **pickled ginger**, finely sliced

1 tablespoon **pickled ginger juice**

duck breasts with bok choy and celeriac

Celeriac is a fabulous vegetable that can be roasted
or steamed and mashed like potatoes. It is also fantastic
grated and served raw with a dressing. Combined with
the flavours in this recipe, it is a magical ingredient
that sits very well with the duck breast and bok choy.

serves four / medium heat / open grill

in the Kitchen

Trim the duck breasts, if necessary, but leave the skin on—this is essential.

Trim, wash and halve the bok choy. Peel and roughly grate the celeriac
and sprinkle with white vinegar.

Combine celeriac, shallots, mayonnaise, ginger and ginger juice. Stir well
and refrigerate, covered, for one hour before use.

at the ⬚Barbecue

Place duck breasts, skin-side-down, on the open grill and cook for three minutes. Do not move them about as you want good clear grill marks on the skin.

Turn duck breasts over where they have been cooking so that the natural fat on the grill will lubricate the bare flesh. Cook for a further four minutes, remove from the heat and rest for five minutes before slicing.

Spray bok choy with oil and place on the barbecue. Cook, turning only once, for one-and-a-half minutes, or until done to your liking. The time may vary, depending on the thickness of the white part of the bok choy. It must remain crunchy.

at the ⬚Table

Place two halves of bok choy in the centre of each plate and spoon some celeriac onto them. Slice duck breasts into rounds and sit on top of the celeriac and bok choy.

chef's note:
The cooking of duck breast is entirely dependent on the depth of flesh. If you are unable to get Muscovy duck breasts, you will probably end up with quite thin ones. Muscovy ducks have an excellent depth of flesh, generally about 2.5–3cm (1–1½in) and sometimes thicker. The cooking time I have recommended will produce medium duck breasts, so cook them for longer if you prefer well-done meat.

8 **quails**

1 tablespoon table **salt**

2 teaspoons ground **white pepper**

2 teaspoons **caster sugar**

1 teaspoon ground **allspice**

1 tablespoon **peanut oil**

220g (7oz) **spinach**, washed and stems removed

¼ cup (60ml/2fl oz) Asian **plum sauce**

salt and pepper quail

with wilted spinach and plum sauce

Quails cook very quickly on the barbecue and, like all game, are best served rare to medium-rare, because with further cooking the meat tends to dry out and lose flavour and texture.

serves four / medium heat / open grill

in the Kitchen

Halve each quail by first cutting through the backbone and then through the breastbone. (Or, buy them ready boned and halved.) Combine salt, pepper, sugar and allspice and mix well.

at the Barbecue

Spray quail halves with oil and cook, skin-side-down, on the open grill for two to three minutes. Spray cut side of quails, turn over and cook for a further three minutes.

Lift from the barbecue and dredge both sides with the salt mixture. Shake off excess salt and pepper and return to the kitchen.

Heat a wok over high heat and pour in the oil. When it starts to smoke, drop spinach into the wok and immediately stir with tongs. Cook for three to four minutes. The spinach will rapidly decrease in volume as it cooks.

at the Table

Serve quails and spinach on individual plates with plum sauce on the side and boiled rice.

red, hot
and meaty

barbecued beef steak stir-fry

One of the great exponents of modern Australian cooking is chef Garry Flynn, formerly of Artis Restaurant in Noosa. He combines flavours beautifully. This is my adaptation for the barbecue of one of his recipes.

serves four / high heat / flat plate

in the Kitchen

Put the meat in a bowl and sprinkle with allspice. Combine soy, mirin, oil, chilli, coriander root and palm sugar. Mix well to dissolve the sugar. Pour over the meat, cover and leave to sit for one hour. Drain the meat, reserving the soy mixture.

at the Barbecue

Spray the flat plate liberally with oil. Add meat strips immediately. Put onions on another part of the sprayed plate and turn both meat and onions regularly for two minutes. Do not combine.

Add bean sprouts and water chestnuts to onions; lift and toss to combine all ingredients, including the meat, in a concentrated area on the barbecue.

Spoon over some of the reserved marinade and lift and toss for another two minutes. Lift into a serving bowl, add the coriander leaves and toss gently.

at the Table

Serve stir-fry with boiled rice or rice noodles.

500g (1 lb) **beef** strips, either rump or sirloin

1 teaspoon ground **allspice**

¼ cup (60ml/2 fl oz) **soy sauce**

1 tablespoon **mirin**

1 tablespoon **peanut oil**, or vegetable oil

1 medium-size **red chilli**, seeded and finely chopped

2 **coriander roots**, washed and finely chopped

1 tablespoon **palm sugar** (jaggery) or dark brown sugar

1 small **onion**, cut into wedges

1 cup **bean sprouts**

8 **water chestnuts**, finely sliced

1 cup loosely packed **coriander** (cilantro) leaves

chef's note:
Buy tender meat for this dish, that is meat that can be cooked quickly and remain tender. Sometimes lesser cuts of meat find their way into stir-fries and they are simply not suitable. I always buy either sirloin or rump and cut it myself into strips about 1cm (½ in) thick.

625g (1¼lb) **rump steak**, cut into 2.5cm (1in) cubes
16 **button mushrooms**, stems removed
and caps wiped clean
8 small **pickled onions**, cut in halves
bamboo or metal **skewers**, 25cm (10in) long
(soak bamboo skewers in water for
30 minutes before using)
1 teaspoon **salt**

barbecued beef kebabs

Kebabs come in all shapes and sizes and under several different names. You will sometimes see them referred to as brochettes, or shishkebabs, but they are only cubes of beef interspersed with vegetable pieces pushed onto skewers and cooked.

serves four / medium heat / open grill

in the Kitchen
Thread the different ingredients onto the skewers, starting and finishing with a cube of beef.

at the Barbecue
Spray the kebabs with oil and cook on the open grill for two minutes on each of four sides, eight minutes in all—you will have turned your kebabs three times. Sprinkle with salt as you turn. Lift kebabs from the barbecue onto a serving plate.

at the Table
These are best served with a salad and some good relishes.

chef's note:
Mushroom growers recommend that mushrooms should not be washed
unless they are to be used immediately. The best way to clean mushrooms,
if they need to be cleaned, is to wipe them individually and gently with a damp cloth.

barbecued lamb sandwich

For many years I served lamb sandwiches at an annual music festival—they were a great hit. It was easy enough to do for 500 people so imagine how simple it will be for you to make them just for four.

serves four / high heat / open grill

in the Kitchen
Sprinkle lamb steaks on both sides with cracked lemon pepper. Slice flat bread pieces in halves.

To prepare sandwich spread, combine mayonnaise, chives and chilli sauce and mix well.

at the Barbecue
Spray lamb steaks with oil and cook on the open grill for two minutes. Turn and cook for one minute longer.

Spray bread with oil and cook, cut-side-down, on the open grill. Check regularly to see that the bread is getting crisp and brown.

at the Table
To assemble each sandwich, spread each base piece of bread with some of the mayonnaise mixture. Put each on a plate and distribute the lettuce and tomatoes on top of the bases. Place the lamb on the tomatoes and then the bocconcini.

Spread some mayonnaise mixture on top pieces of bread and sit these on the bocconcini. Press each sandwich gently and cut on the diagonal.

4 x 125g (4oz) **lamb steaks**

1 tablespoon cracked **lemon pepper**

flat bread, such as ciabatta or Turkish pide, cut into four pieces of similar size to the steaks

4 large **Cos lettuce** leaves, crisp and roughly sliced

16 pieces of **semi-roasted or sun-dried tomatoes**, drained if dried and in oil

2 **bocconcini**, sliced into flat rounds

FOR THE SANDWICH SPREAD

1 cup (250ml/8fl oz) **mayonnaise**

30g (1oz) **garlic chives**, finely chopped

1 tablespoon **hot chilli sauce**

4 **baby eggplants**, about 90g (2oz) each
2 tablespoons dark **soy sauce**
2 tablespoons light **olive oil**
1 tablespoon **honey**
½ teaspoon freshly ground **black pepper**
12 trimmed **lamb cutlets**, each 2cm (¾in) thick
1 teaspoon **salt**

lamb cutlets
with soy and honey eggplant

Lamb cutlets have always been a natural on the barbecue. Served in racks of several cutlets, they became fashionable in restaurants in the '80s. However, in this recipe they are cooked quickly over high heat so they remain succulent and pink in the centre.

serves four / high heat / flat plate and open grill

in the Kitchen
Top and tail eggplant and slice in half lengthwise. Score the flesh by making diagonal cuts to form diamond shapes, being careful not to cut through the skin
  Mix the soy, oil, honey and pepper.

at the Barbecue
Brush soy mixture on the cut side of the eggplant halves, ensuring that some penetrates down into the scored flesh.
  Spray the flat plate with oil and cook eggplant halves, cut-side-down, for two minutes. Turn and cook for a further one minute.
  At the same time, cook cutlets on the open grill for two minutes on each side, sprinkling with salt when you turn them.

at the Table
Place two eggplant halves, cut-side-up, on each plate. Stack three lamb cutlets adjacent to the eggplant and serve with salads of your choice.

125g (4oz) **celery**, finely sliced on the diagonal

90g (3oz) **carrot**, peeled and trimmed,
cut into strips/batons

1 medium **onion**, peeled, halved
and cut into thin wedges

8 good thick **beef sausages**,
each weighing about 90g (3oz)

¼ cup (60ml/2fl oz) **garlic oil**

½ teaspoon dried crushed **chilli**

1 cup of mung **bean sprouts**

¼ cup (60ml/2fl oz) **mirin**

beef sausages

and barbecued vegetable stir-fry

Real sausages make a gourmet statement, well, they try to, anyway. They are, like rissoles, all-time favourites and it's virtually impossible to serve a dud meal of sausages.

serves four / high heat—flat plate / medium heat—open grill

in the Kitchen
Assemble all the vegetables in individual lots on a plate.

at the Barbecue
Cook the sausages on the open grill over medium heat, turning every minute, for seven minutes.

When the sausages have been cooking for two minutes, start the stir-fry. Pour half the oil onto the flat plate over high heat and add celery, carrot and onion. With two spatulas lift and toss the vegetables around the plate, keeping them in a concentrated area just as you do in a wok.

Cook like this for one minute, add the chilli and continue to toss and cook for a further two minutes. Add bean sprouts, remaining oil and the mirin and continue to cook for another two minutes. Be careful here as the mirin will evaporate causing steam that can easily burn you. Lift the cooked vegetables onto a platter. Top with sausages.

at the Table
Serve this dish with steaming fragrant rice.

410g (13oz) **green beans**

1 x 345g (11oz) **sweet potato**

about 20cm (8in) long and 6cm ($2\frac{1}{2}$in) in diameter

1 small **Spanish onion** (red onion), peeled and finely diced

$\frac{1}{2}$ cup (125ml/4fl oz) traditional **vinaigrette**

(see recipe page 139. Make double the quantity.)

8 **lamb loin chops**, each about 90g (3oz) and 2cm ($\frac{3}{4}$in) thick

mushroom oil (see recipe page 136), to serve

lamb chops
with green bean salad and sweet potato

Sweet potato, cooked in a variety of ways, has become a favourite of mine. Combining this lovely vegetable with a salad of green beans and topping with the lamb makes a delicious lunch.

serves four / medium heat—open grill / high heat—flat plate

in the Kitchen

Top and tail the green beans, place in bowl and pour on boiling water to cover. Leave for one minute. Strain and run them under very cold water until beans return to room temperature.

Trim sweet potato if it has thin ends and cook whole in the microwave on high for five minutes.

at the Barbecue

Spray sweet potato with oil and cook on the open grill over medium heat, turning every five minutes, for 30 minutes.

Tip beans onto the flat plate over high heat to heat through—keep them moving and do not let them brown. Lift the beans from the barbecue to a bowl, add onion and vinaigrette and toss to coat all the beans.

Place chops on the open grill—note there is no need to spray—and cook for three minutes on each side, or until done to your liking. (Thicker chops will take longer; thinner ones less time.)

at the Table

Slice the potato, which will now be crusty on the outside, into even rounds and place some in the centre of each plate. Top with portions of green bean salad and sit two of the lamb loin chops adjacent. Pour 1 teaspoon of mushroom oil over the chops.

500g (1lb) lean **minced beef**

1 cup dried **breadcrumbs**

1 small **onion**, finely chopped

1 tablespoon finely chopped **fresh ginger**

1 tablespoon chopped **chervil**, or oregano

1 teaspoon **salt**

juice and finely grated rind of 1 **orange**

1 large **egg,** beaten

2 tablespoons seeded **Dijon mustard**

homemade **barbecue sauce** (see recipe page 133), to serve

orange-scented meatloaf

This meatloaf cooks so well and easily on the barbecue that
you will wonder why you ever bothered with the oven variety.

serves four / medium heat / flat plate

chef's note:

If your foil is thin, layer two or three
sheets to avoid leaks. Always wrap
with the shiny side in when using
foil because that side reflects heat.

in the [K]itchen

Combine all ingredients and, using your hands or a fork, mix thoroughly.

Take a large sheet of thick foil and spray with olive oil. Tip the
mixture onto the foil and shape into a large sausage about 23cm (9in)
long and 6cm (2½in) in diameter.

Wrap the foil around to hold the meat in place and twist the ends
to seal. Refrigerate for at least one hour.

at the [B]arbecue

Cook the loaf on the flat plate for 40 minutes, turning every
10 minutes to ensure even cooking.

Remove from barbecue and leave to rest for 10 minutes
before peeling away the foil.

at the [T]able

Slice and serve with a salad and homemade barbecue sauce.

pork sausages
with spiced apple and redcurrant jelly

I well remember when pork sausages disappeared as you cooked them—they cooked away to nothing as the fat melted. Today the story is different. Sausages retain their shape and their flavour is as good as ever.

serves four / medium heat / flat plate and open grill

1 teaspoon **ground cloves**

1 teaspoon **ground ginger**

1 teaspoon **ground cinnamon**

1 teaspoon **icing sugar**

2 **red apples**, cored and sliced into rounds 1cm (½in) thick

8 good thick **pork sausages**, each about 90g (3oz)

2 cups **mushroom ragoût** (see recipe page 103)

2 tablespoons **redcurrant jelly**, to serve

in the Kitchen
Combine spices with icing sugar and mix well. Press apple slices into spice mix to coat on both sides.

at the Barbecue
Cook pork sausages on the open grill, turning every minute, for nine minutes.

Spray the flat plate with oil and cook apple slices for one minute. Spray and turn apple slices and cook for a further two minutes. Lift off the barbecue onto a warm platter. (Even if the sausages aren't completely cooked yet, the apple slices will retain their heat.)

Take the sausages off the barbecue and place on the same platter. Return to the kitchen and reheat the mushroom ragoût in the microwave on medium for two minutes, stir and microwave for one minute more.

at the Table
Spoon redcurrant jelly over the apple slices and put the platter in the centre of the table.

Serve mushroom ragoût in a separate bowl. Lots of good crusty bread, or even garlic bread, would be great with this meal.

rissoles

Rissoles come in many shapes, sizes and variations, but I have never served them without someone at the table screaming, 'Rissoles—I love 'em!' They remain a perennial favourite that uses economical minced meats.

serves four / medium heat / flat plate and open grill

in the Kitchen

Heat oil and butter in a pan until foaming and fry onion gently for two minutes. Tip onion into a large bowl and add rolled oats, beef, tomato sauce, Tabasco, eggs, salt and pepper. Using your hands, mix well (this is the best way). Refrigerate mixture for one hour.

With wet hands, shape mixture into eight patties, each about 2.5cm (1in) thick, and put on a plate.

at the Barbecue

Spray the flat plate with oil and cook rissoles for one minute, then spray the rissoles with oil, turn over and cook on second side for another minute. Flip them onto the open grill and cook for a further two minutes on each side, or until done to your liking. Cooking time will vary with the thickness of the rissoles.

Meanwhile, spray mushrooms with oil on the gill side (the brown underneath part) first and cook, turning regularly, on the open grill for the same time as the rissoles.

at the Table

Place two rissoles on each plate and top each with a mushroom.

Serve with a little lemon and mustard butter and a salad of your choice.

2 tablespoons **vegetable oil**

1 tablespoon **butter**

1 **small onion**, finely chopped

125g (4oz) **rolled oats**

750g (1½lb) finely **minced beef**

2 tablespoons **tomato sauce**

½ teaspoon **Tabasco sauce**

2 large **eggs**, beaten lightly

½ teaspoon **salt**

1 teaspoon freshly ground **black pepper**

8 medium-size **shiitake mushrooms**, stems removed

lemon and mustard butter (see recipe page 134), to serve

500g (1lb) boneless **loin of lamb**
(ask your butcher to cut it crosswise into 4 steaks)
2 tablespoons extra virgin **olive oil**
2 **parsnips**, each about 220g (7oz)
2 **Roma** (plum) **tomatoes**, cut in half lengthwise
¼ teaspoon **salt**
1 **butternut pumpkin**, about 750g (24oz)
balsamic vinegar

loin of lamb
with roma tomatoes and butternut pumpkin

Butternut pumpkin is a perfect partner for lamb.
This member of the squash family is remarkably versatile—
try it in pickles or, mashed, as the basis for soufflés and
scones. Roma tomatoes, sometimes called egg tomatoes,
are superb for both their flavour and structure.

serves four / medium heat—flat plate / high heat—open grill

in the K**itchen**

Trim lamb steaks, place in a bowl and pour olive oil over to coat.

Peel parsnips and cut off any of the fibrous end pieces. Cut each
into four wedges and remove the woody core. Sprinkle the cut side
of the tomatoes with salt.

Cut the pumpkin in half lengthwise. Cover one half with plastic wrap
and refrigerate for another use. Cook remaining half, with seeds still in,
in the microwave on high for seven minutes.

at the Barbecue

Spray cut side of pumpkin with oil and cook on the open grill over high heat for five minutes. Turn over and leave to cook for 10 minutes. Scoop out the seeds at this stage with a spoon taking care as the pumpkin will be hot.

Spray parsnips with oil and cook on the open grill over high heat for four minutes. Lift parsnip onto the flat plate and cook over medium heat for a further four minutes, turning regularly. Turn over the pumpkin again and leave to cook for 10 minutes.

Spray cut side of tomato halves with oil and cook, cut-side-down, on the flat plate for two minutes. Turn and cook for two minutes more.

Cook oiled lamb steaks on the flat plate over medium heat for four minutes on each side. Rest for four minutes before slicing and serving.

at the Table

Collect all the barbecued ingredients onto a large platter and return to the kitchen.

Slice pumpkin into eight even portions and place two pieces in the centre of each plate. Sit two pieces of parsnip on top of the pumpkin and top with a half tomato, cut-side-up.

Cut lamb on the diagonal and place two pieces on each plate, standing them against the stacked vegetables. Sprinkle with a little balsamic vinegar and serve immediately.

500g (1lb) boneless **loin of lamb**

12 slices **Desiree potatoes**, cut in rounds 2cm (¾in) thick and par-boiled for 5 minutes

220g (7oz) **spinach leaves**, washed, dried and stemmed

125g (4oz) **croutons**

1 cup (250ml/8fl oz) **Caesar dressing**, purchased

2 rashers rindless **bacon**, cut into 2.5cm (1in) lengths

loin lamb butterflies
with potato and spinach 'caesar'

I first became aware of this invaluable cut of meat while working for a stylish catering company in the early '90s.

serves four / high heat / flat plate

in the Kitchen

Cut loin of lamb into eight even-sized pieces. Cut each piece almost through and open out into a butterfly shape, about 2cm (¾in) thick and weighing about 60g (2oz) each. Put the spinach in a bowl and refrigerate to crisp.

at the Barbecue

Spray potato slices with oil and cook on the flat plate for two minutes. Spray with oil, turn and cook for two to three minutes more. Put bacon on at the same time as the potatoes and cook for four to five minutes, or until crisp. Lift bacon onto paper towel to drain.

   When you have turned the potatoes for the first time, spray the flat side of each lamb butterfly with oil and cook on the flat plate for two minutes. Spray with oil, turn over and cook for a further three minutes. It is important that as you turn each lamb steak you hold it in place for a couple of seconds by pressing on top with a spatula. This stops the lamb from curling up. You may like to skewer the lamb in place with a toothpick before you start cooking.

at the Table

Place three slices of potato in the centre of each plate. Top with two lamb butterflies. Add bacon and croutons to spinach and pour on dressing. Lift and toss leaves to coat before serving.

410g (13oz) **pork fillet,** trimmed

315g (10oz) medium dried **spaghetti**

90g (3oz) **zucchini**, finely sliced into rounds

90g (3oz) **white onion**, sliced in rings

2 cloves **garlic**, peeled and crushed

$^2/_3$ cup (150ml/5fl oz) **white wine**

1 tablespoon freshly chopped **Italian parsley**

1 teaspoon freshly chopped **marjoram**

$^1/_2$ teaspoon **salt**

$^1/_2$ teaspoon cracked **black pepper**

1 tablespoon extra virgin **olive oil**

pork fillet
with zucchini and spaghetti

It seems as if there's nothing you can't cook on a barbecue—
well, all right, a soufflé or a sponge may present a bit of
a challenge. But this dish demonstrates the versatility
of the barbecue plate by reheating cooked spaghetti
and combining it with other flavours.

serves four / high heat / flat plate

in the Kitchen

Slice pork fillet into rounds 2cm ($^3/_4$in) thick and flatten with your hand to about half the thickness.

  Bring a large pot of salted water to the boil and drop in the spaghetti. To cook *al dente* takes about eight to nine minutes, but in this case, the pasta must not be overcooked. When just done, strain and run under warm water. If you use it straight away there is no need to rub oil through the spaghetti.

at the Barbecue

Spray pork fillet pieces with oil and cook on the flat plate for two minutes on each side. At the same time, add zucchini, onion and garlic to another part of the oiled plate. Cook vegetables, moving them around, for three minutes.

When pork is cooked combine it with the vegetables and add the spaghetti. Pour over half the wine and, using two spatulas, lift and combine spaghetti with meat and vegetable mixture. Cook like this for a further three minutes and add remaining wine.

Sprinkle with parsley, marjoram, salt and pepper, lifting and tossing to spread the flavours through the spaghetti. Make sure you scrape up the tasty caramelised pieces while turning the vegetables and spaghetti.

at the Table

Lift the cooked ingredients into a big bowl, drizzle with olive oil and serve with a salad of your choice and crusty bread.

4 marbled **sirloin steaks**,
each 5cm (2in) thick
salt and freshly ground **black pepper**

perfectly barbecued beef steak

No barbecue cookbook is complete without a definitive recipe for cooking steak. After many years of barbecuing beef steak, I know this is the best method. Choosing the correct cut of beef is crucial to the final result and never cook it past medium-rare.

serves four / high heat—flat plate / medium heat—open grill

chef's note:
You will notice that I recommend leaving some fat on the steak. This is essential for flavour complexity. If you don't wish to eat the fat, slice it off after the steak is cooked. To identify marbled beef, look for streaks of white through the red meat— these are thin lines of fat that melt during the cooking process giving barbecued beef steak its superb flavour.

in the Kitchen

Trim fat from your steaks but be sure to leave at least 0.5cm (¼in).

at the Barbecue

Spray steaks with oil and place on the flat plate over high heat. Cook for two minutes without disturbing the meat. Use tongs for handling. Do not at any time puncture the steaks with forks or knives, because you will release the meat's vital juices.

Spray steaks lightly with oil and turn over onto another part of the very hot flat barbecue plate. Do not lift the steak and turn it onto the place where it has been cooking because the intensity of the heat will have gone. Cook for a further two minutes.

Flip the steaks again, but this time onto the open grill over medium heat, and cook for three minutes on each side, sprinkling with salt and pepper as you turn. Lift onto a warm platter and rest for five minutes before serving (this gives the juices a chance to settle).

at the Table

Serve steak on individual plates with vegetables, or a salad of your choice, and at least one good mustard.

4 large **bread rolls**

500g (1lb) **minced veal**

250g (8oz) **cooked ham**, very finely chopped

2 **eggs**

1 teaspoon **Tabasco sauce**

1 tablespoon **tomato sauce**

60g (2oz) **onion**, finely diced

½ teaspoon **salt**

dried **breadcrumbs**, if necessary

4 medium-size field **mushrooms**

2 cups shredded **lettuce**

FOR THE BEETROOT RELISH

220g (7oz) **beetroot**, cooked, cooled and skins removed

2 **salad onions** (scallion), finely chopped

1 teaspoon **anchovy sauce**

1 tablespoon white **wine vinegar**

2 teaspoons **truffle oil**, or walnut oil

veal and ham burgers
with beetroot relish

It would be impossible to write a barbecue cookbook without a hamburger recipe. This one got an airing on a TV programme and instantly proved extremely popular.

serves four / medium heat—flat plate / high heat—open grill

in the Kitchen

Cut bread rolls in half horizontally and pull out the soft centre of each half to make a well.

  Combine veal, ham, eggs, Tabasco, tomato sauce, onions, salt and the bread removed from the buns, broken into really small pieces. Using your hands, mix well. The bread you have used should be enough to bind the mixture, but if it is too moist, add enough dried breadcrumbs to take up any excess liquid. Shape into four even-size patties—cover and refrigerate.

Make relish by grating the beetroot roughly. Combine with salad onions, anchovy sauce, vinegar and oil and mix well. Leftover relish will keep, refrigerated, for about one week.

at the Barbecue

Spray patties with oil and cook on the flat plate over medium heat for one minute. Spray again, turn and cook the second side for another minute.

Spray mushrooms on the gill side (the brown underneath part) and cook on the open grill over high heat for two minutes on each side.

Lift hamburger patties onto the open grill and cook over high heat for a further three minutes on each side, or until done to your liking. (The time recommended will give you medium-rare patties.)

Spray insides of hamburger buns with oil and cook, cut-side-down, on the open grill for 30 seconds. Turn to cook for 30 seconds on the other side.

Lift all ingredients from the barbecue and assemble by putting equal portions of lettuce in the base part of each bread roll. Add a cooked pattie and top with a mushroom.

at the Table

Spoon beetroot relish on top of the mushrooms and add the top part of the bread roll. Press down to compress the fillings and serve with your choice of salads.

chef's note:
When bread rolls are left flat, fillings can easily slide out as you bite. I adopted the habit of scooping out the centres of the bread rolls after seeing many such disasters. If you make a well on each side, the fillings are held in much better. You can also serve the beetroot relish with cold meats and other barbecued meats.

venison sausages
with parsnip mash and cumberland sauce

There are many versions of this lovely old-fashioned sauce, which is great with boiled meats and game terrines. I have adapted this variation specially to serve with venison sausages.

serves four / medium heat / flat plate

in the Kitchen

Chop parsnips and potatoes to a similar size, cover with water and bring to the boil. Simmer until tender. Strain and return to saucepan. Add butter and cheese, cover and leave to sit for three minutes. Roughly mash the vegetables, scoop into a microwave-proof bowl, cover and set aside.

For the Cumberland sauce, combine redcurrant jelly, mustard, ginger and rind and mix well. Cook in a microwave on high for 30 seconds. Remove and mix thoroughly. This process may take longer if the jelly has come straight from the refrigerator. Leave to sit at room temperature.

at the Barbecue

Spray sausages with oil and cook on the flat plate, turning every minute, for six minutes. Lift from the barbecue and leave to rest for four minutes before serving.

at the Table

Reheat parsnip mash in the microwave on medium for two minutes, remove and stir, then microwave for two minutes longer. Spoon a portion onto each plate. Lean two sausages against the mash. Serve the Cumberland sauce separately with green vegetables of your choice.

410g (13oz) **parsnips**, peeled, quartered lengthwise and core removed

90g (3oz) **waxy potatoes**, peeled

90g (3oz) **butter**

90g (3oz) **Stilton cheese**, at room temperature

8 **venison sausages**, each about 100g (3oz)

FOR THE CUMBERLAND SAUCE

75g (2½oz) **redcurrant jelly**, or quince jelly

1 tablespoon prepared **English mustard**

¼ teaspoon **ground ginger**

1 teaspoon finely grated **orange rind**

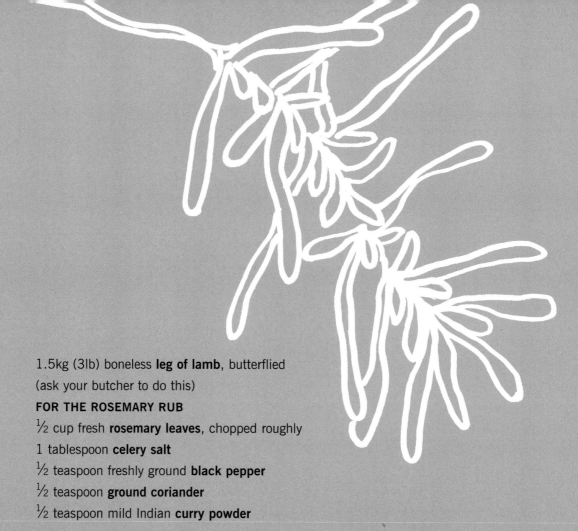

1.5kg (3lb) boneless **leg of lamb**, butterflied
(ask your butcher to do this)

FOR THE ROSEMARY RUB

½ cup fresh **rosemary leaves**, chopped roughly

1 tablespoon **celery salt**

½ teaspoon freshly ground **black pepper**

½ teaspoon **ground coriander**

½ teaspoon mild Indian **curry powder**

boneless leg of lamb
with rosemary rub

I was so accustomed to leg of lamb on the bone that when I first had this boneless variation I was very excited about its possibilities. A boneless leg is stunning spread and lightly marinated with tandoori paste, but in the following recipe the natural flavours of the lamb are highlighted by the rub.

serves four / medium heat / open grill

in the Kitchen

Lay the leg of lamb out, skin-side-down, as flat as possible and ensure that the meat has an even thickness. This can be difficult as the muscle structure varies and you may have to slice off the thicker meat to make it flat. Push two or three skewers across it to maintain its flat appearance.

Combine rosemary, salt, pepper, coriander and curry powder and mix well. With your fingers, sprinkle and spread half the rub ingredients over the cut side of the lamb and massage it in.

at the Barbecue

Cook the leg of lamb, cut-side-down, on the open grill for five minutes.

Spray skin side of lamb with oil and turn the leg over to cook for 10 minutes. Spray cut side with a little oil and sprinkle with the remaining rub, using a spatula to press it into the meat. Turn meat over and cook for five minutes longer.

Continue to cook the meat, turning at intervals, for 25 minutes more, or until done to your liking.

at the Table

Lift meat from the barbecue and leave in a warm place to rest for 10 minutes. Slice and serve with salads or vegetables of your choice. Lamb cooked this way is also delicious chilled and served with a salad or in sandwiches.

chef's note:
When meat rests after cooking, the juices settle and the meat carves
more easily. The juices that collect in the base of the platter can
be spooned over the sliced meat.

perfect
partners

corn on the cob with parsley pesto

Native Americans knew about corn, a real culinary treasure, centuries ago and it was ultimately taken to Europe for us all to share. This recipe concentrates on combining great new flavours.

serves four / medium heat / open grill

4 **cobs of corn**, including husk and silk
FOR THE PARSLEY PESTO
1 cup **parsley** sprigs, washed and tightly packed
30g (1oz) unsalted **macadamia nuts**, roughly chopped and roasted
100ml (3fl oz) **macadamia nut oil**
2 large cloves **garlic**, peeled and crushed
60g (2oz) **cheddar cheese**, grated

in the Kitchen
Pull back the husk (the green outer part) on each cob and remove the silky fibres. Pull husk back over the corn.

For the pesto, purée all ingredients in a food processor or blender until smooth. (Pulse the processor until the ingredients start to break down, then leave the engine running until a smooth paste forms.)

at the Barbecue
Cook corn on the open grill, turning every five minutes, for 30 minutes. Spray with water if it looks as if the husks are drying out too much. Remove from the barbecue and allow to cool for five minutes.

at the Table
Pull husks back from the corn (snip off, if desired)—be careful not to burn yourself as the steam escapes from under the husks. Spread with pesto and serve immediately.

barbecued potatoes
with 'tonnato' dressing

Waxy potatoes are essential for this style of dish, so look for ones with creamy yellow flesh, such as Wilja or Duke of York. By the way, the dressing can be used for a number of dishes, including its traditional partner, cold poached veal.

serves four / medium heat / flat plate

6–8 **waxy potatoes**, about 410g (13oz)
125g (4oz) **celery**, finely diced
60g (2oz) **onion**, finely diced
8 **capers**, halved
1 tablespoon **rosemary**, dried and crumbled

FOR THE DRESSING
155g (5oz) **canned tuna**, drained
4 **anchovy** fillets
1½ cups (375ml/12fl oz) **mayonnaise**
1 tablespoon **white vinegar**
½ teaspoon **salt**
¼ teaspoon **white pepper**

chef's note:
You may like to sprinkle drained capers over this dish for presentation, but there is plenty of flavour here already.

in the Kitchen

Wash potatoes and cut in half lengthwise. Cover with water, bring to the boil, and simmer for five minutes. Strain and cool.

To make the dressing, blend all ingredients to a smooth, creamy consistency.

at the Barbecue

Spray cut side of potatoes with oil and cook on the flat plate for two minutes. Turn over and cook for a further two minutes. Test the potatoes to see if they are cooked by piercing with a skewer or sharp knife—if it slides easily through the potatoes, they are ready.

Lift potatoes from barbecue onto a platter. Return to the kitchen.

at the Table

Sprinkle celery and onion over the potatoes. Distribute capers evenly around and sprinkle with dried rosemary.

Spoon tuna sauce over the potatoes. Shake the platter to ensure that the sauce sinks through to the bottom. Cover with plastic wrap and refrigerate for at least four hours before serving.

60g (2oz) **butter**

60g (2oz) **salad onions** (scallion), peeled and chopped

3 cloves **garlic**, peeled and very finely chopped

410g (13oz) assorted **mushrooms**, roughly chopped
(use wild or exotic mushrooms if available)

1¼ cups (310ml/10fl oz) **demi-glace**
(available from delicatessens)

¼ cup (60ml/2fl oz) **red wine**

1 tablespoon freshly chopped **marjoram**

½ teaspoon **salt**

mushroom ragoût

I have used this recipe so many times I have lost count.
It is an absolute beauty and you can serve this dish for
breakfast, lunch or dinner.

serves four

in the Kitchen

Melt butter in a saucepan and cook salad onions and garlic for two minutes.
Add mushrooms, demi-glace and red wine and bring to the boil. Reduce heat
and simmer for at least one hour.

Add marjoram and salt and cook for 10 minutes more. Serve at once.

4 **Roma** (plum) **tomatoes**

220g (7oz) **mesclun leaves**

(mixed baby salad leaves)

125g (4oz) **goat's cheese**, crumbled or diced

½ cup (125ml / 4fl oz) **barbecued garlic dressing**

(see recipe page 128), to serve

mesclun leaves

with goat cheese and barbecued garlic dressing

Goat cheese is certainly a part of every Frenchman's way of life and I well remember seeing a vast array of shapes, sizes and textures in Périgord, France. But now delicious goat cheese is made in many countries—for this recipe try ticklemore, made in Devon, or golden cross from Wessex.

serves four / high heat / open grill

in the Kitchen

Cut tomatoes in half.

Arrange leaves in a salad bowl and top with crumbled goat cheese.
(Remove the crusty skin of the cheese if you wish, but I like to leave it on.)

at the Barbecue

Spray tomatoes with oil and cook on the open grill for one-and-a-half minutes on each side. Lift from the barbecue and allow to cool for 10 minutes.

at the Table

Scatter tomatoes over salad leaves and serve. Pass the barbecued garlic dressing separately.

500g (1lb) **eggplant**

2 teaspoons **salt**

¼ cup (60ml/2 fl oz) **olive oil**

1 **Spanish onion**, peeled and sliced thinly

1 red, green or yellow **capsicum** (bell pepper),
seeded, cored and roughly diced

2 cloves **garlic**, peeled and roughly chopped

2 ripe **tomatoes**, roughly chopped

2 medium **zucchinis**, roughly diced

2 teaspoons chopped fresh **thyme leaves**

1 teaspoon freshly chopped **oregano**

¼ cup (60ml/2fl oz) **vegetable stock**

½ teaspoon freshly ground **black pepper**

2 tablespoons freshly chopped **parsley** or **basil**

4 medium **pitta breads**

barbecued
pitta bread with ratatouille

Ratatouille is a super vegetable stew which can
be served hot or cool. It freezes well and is the
base for wonderful winter soups.

serves four / medium heat / open grill

in the K̲itchen

Roughly chop the eggplant, place in a colander, sprinkle liberally
with salt and allow to drain for 30 minutes.

Heat olive oil in a large frying pan over medium heat. Add onion and fry for
about three minutes, or until soft. Add capsicum, garlic, tomatoes and zucchini
and stir well. Mix in thyme and oregano.

Rinse eggplant under cold water and pat dry with paper towels; tumble into the
rest of the ingredients along with the stock. Stir, cover and simmer over low heat.
Cook, stirring occasionally, for 20 to 30 minutes. Season to taste with pepper and simmer
for a further 10 minutes. Spoon into a serving dish and sprinkle with parsley or basil.

Take the pitta breads and cut each into six triangles of similar size.

at the B̲arbecue

Spray each piece of pitta bread lightly with oil and cook on the open grill for 30 seconds.
Again spray with oil, turn over and cook for a further 30 seconds to one minute, or until crisp.

at the T̲able

Place the ratatouille, hot, warm or at room temperature, in the centre of the
table with a bowl of crisped bread and let everyone help themselves.

chef's note:
Ratatouille is best made the day before it is to be used. If it is not all devoured,
it will keep perfectly well, refrigerated, in a sealed container for up to five days.

2 Beurre Bosch **pears**

1 **lemon**, halved

125g (4oz) **gorgonzola**, crumbled or diced

220g (7oz) **spinach leaves**,
washed, stems removed, crisped

8 slices **pancetta**

saffron threads

2 tablespoons extra virgin **olive oil**

1 tablespoon red **wine vinegar**

barbecued pear
with pancetta, gorgonzola and spinach salad

The best pears for this recipe are the brown-skinned Beurre Bosch. They are firm fleshed when ripe. However, if they are not in season, use any firm pear. The salad uses saffron threads which, like diamonds, are expensive but a worthwhile investment.

serves four / medium heat / open grill

in the Kitchen

Halve pears lengthwise and remove stems and seeds. (This is best done with a Parisienne cutter and a sharp knife.) Slice pears into lengths 1cm (½in) thick. If you are not doing the barbecuing immediately, rub each slice with lemon to prevent browning.

Put cheese and spinach leaves in a salad bowl, cover and refrigerate.

at the Barbecue

Cook pancetta on the open grill, turning regularly, until crisp.

The pears must be 'flash' barbecued, just to bring out some extra flavour, so spray the slices with the smallest amount of oil and cook them on the open grill for just 30 seconds on each side.

Lift pears from the barbecue to a warm platter and sprinkle immediately with two good pinches of saffron threads. Take pears and pancetta to the kitchen and arrange on top of the cheese and spinach.

at the Table

Drizzle the salad with olive oil and red wine vinegar and serve at once.

60g (2oz) **butter**

1 small **onion**, chopped

1 clove **garlic**, chopped

2 tablespoons finely chopped **parsley**

375g (12oz) Italian **arborio rice**

4 cups (1L/32fl oz)

chicken stock, simmering

2 teaspoons **salt**

½ teaspoon **white pepper**

155g (5oz) **Parmesan cheese**, freshly grated

basic risotto

A bowl of risotto is wonderful in its own right, but the variations you can achieve with a basic risotto, or with leftover risotto, are amazing. For something a little different, turn cooked risotto into a springform tin and allow to set overnight. Cut it into wedges and char-grill or pan-fry.

makes about 900g (1¾lb) of risotto

in the Kitchen

Melt half the butter in a large, heavy saucepan and fry onion and garlic.

When onion is soft and golden, add parsley and cook over low heat for two minutes. Add rice and fry for three minutes, stirring constantly to coat grains. Add 1 cup (250ml/8fl oz) boiling stock and cook gently until it is absorbed, stirring all the time.

Increase the heat to medium and continue to cook for 15–20 minutes, stirring constantly and adding the remaining stock gradually, until the rice is tender and all the liquid is absorbed.

Season to taste with salt and pepper, stir in cheese and the remaining butter.

Cover with a lid and leave risotto to sit for three minutes before serving.

at the Table

You could serve this as an excellent side dish on its own, or with a little extra grated Parmesan cheese.

beetroot

500g (1lb) large **beetroots**

4 **blood oranges**

2 tablespoons **Dijon mustard**

2 tablespoons chopped **parsley**

2 teaspoons **caraway seeds**, toasted

with blood oranges and mustard dressing

Beetroot are sensational roasted, baked or boiled. Combine them with oranges for a great salad. Blood oranges not only make a great visual impact but their flavour is a little different from regular oranges, which can be used, however, when blood oranges are unavailable.

serves four

in the Kitchen

Cover beetroots with cold water, bring to the boil and simmer for one hour. Leave in the cooking liquid to cool. Remove skins when cool enough to handle.

Peel three of the oranges to reveal the flecked flesh. Slice into rounds, catching as much of the juice as possible, and set aside. Juice the remaining orange and combine with reserved juices. Mix juice with Dijon mustard.

Slice the beetroot into rounds 1cm (½in) thick and layer alternately with the orange rounds to create a spiral effect.

at the Table

Sprinkle parsley and caraway seeds over the top of the beetroot and orange and spoon on the orange mustard mixture.

410g (13oz) of fresh **green pawpaw**, finely shredded

½ cup fresh **mint** leaves, washed

½ cup fresh **coriander** (cilantro) leaves, washed

¼ cup snipped **garlic chives**

1 tablespoon finely shredded **Kaffir lime leaves**

1 tablespoon **red chilli**, seeded and finely diced

½ cup (125ml/4fl oz) **nam jim dressing** (see recipe page 131)

green pawpaw salad

I first saw this salad in Bangkok on a street stall. It delivers all those marvellous Thai flavours that surprise the palate yet leave it beautifully refreshed.

serves four

in the K̲itchen

Combine all ingredients and stir well. Serve immediately.

500g (1lb) **onions**, peeled and sliced into rings
1 tablespoon **oil**
30g (1oz) **butter**
about $1\frac{1}{4}$ cups (300ml/10fl oz) **beer**

dad's barbecued onions

My Dad's barbecued onions are famous, well, I think so.
They have been a part of his barbecue repertoire for
as long as I can remember him cooking family meals
for us, about 45 years.

serves four / medium heat / flat plate

chef's note:
While I don't cover my onions
to cook them like my Dad did, they
still taste fantastic (though not
as delicious as his). Perhaps his
secret was the old enamel pie
dish he covered them with,
or is that just sentimentality?

in the Kitchen
Sprinkle onions with a little salt, if you wish.

at the Barbecue
Melt butter and oil on the flat plate and add the onions. Move them around on the plate with a spatula and let them brown lightly. Pour about a third of the beer over the onions and stir.
   Dad always used to cover his onions with an old enamel pie dish. If you feel it is necessary to cover them, use a wok or saucepan lid to keep the moisture in. I don't cover mine. Leave the onions to stew in their own juices and add the remaining beer as they start to become dry.

at the Table
Lift the browned and beery onions into a bowl and serve with any grilled meat or sausages.

4 **baby eggplant**, each about 90g (3oz)

1 teaspoon **salt**

4 **capsicum** (bell pepper) wedges, preferably red

1 tablespoon **sesame seeds**, toasted

1 tablespoon **balsamic vinegar**

1 tablespoon extra virgin **olive oil**

1 teaspoon freshly cracked **black pepper**

eggplant, capsicum and
sesame seed salad

This salad can be used as a vegetarian entrée
as well as an accompaniment to barbecued meats.

serves four / medium heat / open grill

chef's note:
You can buy sesame seeds lightly toasted,
but it is easy to colour them at home by
toasting them over medium heat
in a small frying pan.
The salad can be made a couple of days
ahead and kept, refrigerated, in a covered
container. Serve at room temperature.

in the Kitchen

Remove stems from eggplants, cut in half lengthwise and sprinkle
cut sides with salt. Leave to sit for 30 minutes. Wash eggplants
under cold water and pat dry with paper towel.

at the Barbecue

Spray cut side of each eggplant half with plenty of oil and cook
on the open grill for three minutes on each side. Spray capsicum
wedges on both sides and cook for two minutes on each side.

Take the capsicum and eggplant to the kitchen. Arrange
eggplant halves, in a single layer, on a plate. Cut capsicums into
strips, 1cm (½in) thick, and scatter evenly over the eggplant.

Sprinkle with toasted sesame seeds and drizzle with balsamic
vinegar and olive oil.

at the Table

Sprinkle with cracked pepper and serve.

sweet
grillings

220g (7oz) **mascarpone**
¼ cup (60ml / 2fl oz) pouring **cream**
2 tablespoons **vanilla sugar**
8 **bananas**, each about 90g (3oz),
not too ripe, peeled
60g (2oz) **butter**, melted
¼ cup (60ml / 2fl oz) **dark rum**

bananas with rum
and whipped mascarpone

Being a Queenslander, I love bananas, naturally. They are an all-time great fruit, nutritionally sound and absolutely delicious.

serves four / medium heat / flat plate

chef's note:
You can buy vanilla sugar at the supermarket, but it's very easy to make. Simply place caster sugar in a glass jar with one or two whole vanilla pods. If you use a vanilla bean to infuse milk for custards, remove it from the milk afterwards, wash and dry it thoroughly and return it to the caster sugar.

in the Kitchen
Whip mascarpone with cream and vanilla sugar.

at the Barbecue
Spread half the melted butter on the flat plate and cook bananas for two minutes. Spoon remaining melted butter over and, using a long spatula and a set of tongs, turn over the bananas gently and cook for two minutes more. Lift onto a platter.

at the Table
Pour rum over the bananas and serve with the whipped mascarpone.

250g (8oz) selected **seasonal fruit**,
seeded and cut into pieces of similar size

4 **bamboo skewers**, soaked for 30 minutes in cold water

60g (2oz) **caster sugar**

FOR THE ORANGE SYRUP

1 cup (250ml/8fl oz) **orange juice**

¼ cup (60ml/2fl oz) **brandy**

60g (2oz) **brown sugar**

12 whole **cloves**

3 **cardamom pods**, squeezed open

skewers of seasonal fruit
with orange syrup

For this recipe, choose seasonal fruits that are firm enough to push onto skewers. In summer, it might be seeded and cubed stone fruit; in winter, apples and pears; in autumn, halved figs. The choice is entirely yours, but take advantage of the wide variety of fruit now imported from around the world.

serves four / medium heat / flat plate

in the Kitchen

Thread pieces of fruit onto the skewers, taking care with fruit such as apples and pears, which brown quickly—prepare them at the last minute and sprinkle them with lemon juice to reduce the browning.

To make the syrup, combine orange juice, brandy, brown sugar, cloves and cardamom pods in a saucepan. Bring to the boil and simmer for 25 minutes. Remove from heat, cool and strain to remove the cloves and cardamom pods.

Check the sweetness, you may like to add a little more sugar to the syrup.

at the Barbecue

Place skewers on the flat plate (it is not necessary to oil it) and sprinkle with some of the caster sugar. Turn the fruit very quickly, sprinkling with sugar as you go. Cook skewers for less than 30 seconds each side maximum. The fruit should not be cooked, just warmed, and the sugar will caramelise but not burn. Lift the skewers and place on a platter.

at the Table

Spoon a little of the orange syrup over the skewers and serve the rest in a jug at the table.

chef's note:
With this dish the variations are endless: halved figs sprinkled with a little sugar and flashed, cut-side-down, on the barbecue are a sensuous and sumptuous thing to eat, especially when topped with a creamy blue cheese.

16 medium-size **strawberries**, hulls removed, halved

30g (1oz) **caster sugar**

¼ cup (60ml/2fl oz) **Grand Marnier**, or Cointreau

1 large **mango**, very ripe

1 cup (250ml/8fl oz) thickened **cream**

4 **crêpes**

icing sugar, for dusting

FOR THE CRÊPE BATTER (MAKES 20 TO 24 CRÊPES)

345g (11oz) **flour**

pinch of **salt**

3 **eggs**, beaten

1½ cups (375ml/12fl oz) **milk**

1 tablespoon **brandy**

2 teaspoons **butter**, melted

extra **butter**, for greasing pan

strawberry crêpes with mango cream

I have always absolutely loved strawberries and, while I prefer to eat them straight from the plant, I rarely see them like that these days. So I enhance the flavour by maceration.

serves four / medium heat / flat plate

in the Kitchen

Sprinkle strawberries with sugar and Grand Marnier and leave to macerate for at least one hour before using. Remove skin from the mango and slice the flesh away from the seed. Purée very finely in a food processor. Whip the cream until stiff, stir in mango purée and refrigerate.

　To make the crêpes, sift flour and salt into a bowl. Make a well in the centre and add eggs and milk. Using a balloon whisk, mix well, drawing in the flour from the sides of the well. Beat until smooth, then stir in brandy and melted butter; cover and stand for one hour. Strain into a jug—the batter should be totally free of lumps.

To cook the crêpes, heat a little butter in an 18cm (7in) crêpe pan and pour off excess. Pour about 1 tablespoon of batter from the jug into the pan, rotating the pan quickly to coat bottom thinly and evenly. Pour off any excess batter.

Heat gently and, when small bubbles appear, use a spatula to flip the crêpe over. Cook for another minute on the second side. Repeat until all batter is used. Keep four crêpes warm, and cool the remainder on wire racks.

at the Barbecue

Lift strawberry halves from the liquid with a slotted spoon and place on the flat plate (it is not necessary to spray the flat plate). Turn very quickly, warming for no longer than one minute in total.

Lift the strawberries from the plate and place eight halves down the centre of each crêpe. Loosely fold crêpes around the strawberries.

at the Table

Spoon remaining liqueur soaking liquid over strawberry crêpes, dust with icing sugar and serve with the mango cream.

chef's note:
Freeze leftover crêpes in handy stacks of six,
interleaved with sheets of plastic wrap.

2 large **Granny Smith apples**, unpeeled
½ tablespoon freshly grated **nutmeg**
1 tablespoon **caster sugar**
60g (2oz) **butter**, melted
30ml (1fl oz) **Calvados**
vanilla ice-cream, to serve

nutmeg apple slices
with calvados and vanilla ice-cream

The best thing about barbecued desserts is that as well as being delicious they are so simple. I suggest you use apple-scented Calvados here, but you can substitute any brandy or Cognac.

serves four / medium heat / flat plate

in the Kitchen
Core apples and slice into rounds about 1cm (½in) thick.
  Combine nutmeg and sugar and sprinkle apple slices
on both sides with nutmeg mixture.

at the Barbecue
Spread half the melted butter on the flat plate and cook apple slices
for one minute. Spoon over the remaining butter, turn over slices and
cook for two minutes longer. Lift onto a platter.

at the Table
Spoon the Calvados over and serve with balls of vanilla ice-cream.

4 slices **raisin bread**, each about 2cm (¾in) thick

3 **eggs**, beaten lightly

1 cup (250ml/8fl oz) **milk**

1 teaspoon **ground cinnamon**

220ml (7fl oz) pouring **cream**, whipped stiffly

¼ cup (60ml/2fl oz) **Cointreau**

60g (2oz) **butter**, melted

icing sugar

cinnamon french toast
with cointreau cream

French toast is one of the great carbohydrate kick-starts to the day, but no rule says you can't also serve it as a dessert.

serves four / medium heat / flat plate

chef's note:
Almost any stewed fruit goes well with this French toast, but one of my favourites is stewed rhubarb and apple, which has a lovely bite that balances the sugar rush.

in the [K]itchen

Remove crusts from the raisin bread (if you wish).

Combine eggs, milk and cinnamon. Mix the whipped cream and Cointreau together and refrigerate.

at the [B]arbecue

Spray flat plate lightly with oil. Dip raisin bread in the egg mixture and cook on the flat plate for one minute.

Turn over raisin bread onto another part of the oiled flat plate and cook for two minutes.

Lift onto a platter, spoon the melted butter over and dredge with icing sugar.

at the [T]able

Serve this special French toast smothered with Cointreau Cream.

barbecue basics

30g (1oz) cloves **garlic**
1 cup (250ml/8fl oz) light **olive oil**
½ teaspoon **salt**
¼ teaspoon freshly ground **black pepper**
1 teaspoon **white sugar**
2 tablespoons (40ml) Spanish **sherry vinegar**

barbecued garlic dressing

When I did a variation of this dressing recently on the 'Today Show', I used roasted garlic. I was surprised by the number of requests for the recipe, so I'm sure this one will become a favourite.

makes about 1¼ cups (310ml/10fl oz) / moderate heat / flat plate

in the Ⓚitchen
If the garlic cloves are large, cut them in half.

at the Ⓑarbecue
Spray the flat plate with oil and cook garlic for four minutes, turning it regularly to allow it to brown lightly. Lift from the barbecue.

Return to the kitchen and process garlic with oil, salt, pepper and sugar in a food processor or blender until smooth and light cream in colour.

With motor running, add vinegar through the feed chute and, when combined, switch off and pour this rich dressing into a screw-top jar. Keeps, refrigerated, for about two weeks.

2 large **egg yolks**, at room temperature
¼ teaspoon **salt**
pinch of **white pepper**
½ teaspoon prepared **mustard** (smooth Dijon is best)
1 teaspoon **white vinegar**
1 cup (250ml/8fl oz) light **olive oil**, or vegetable oil

basic hand-made mayonnaise

You can make this unique sauce in a processor or blender, but I always do it by hand. Something seems to happen when it's mixed with a balloon whisk that gives it just a little extra magic. Once you've tried this mayonnaise you'll never want to use anything else.

makes about 1¼ cups (310ml/10fl oz)

chef's note:
If you add the oil too quickly, the mayonnaise will curdle. If this happens, beat in 1 teaspoon of hot water and continue to add the oil gradually to the mixture. Remember that when you use egg yolks they cook very quickly, so if you are doing a warm egg yolk sauce, such as an hollandaise, and the egg yolks look as if they will curdle, drop a small ice cube into the mixture and whisk away from the heat.

in the Ⓚitchen

Place egg yolks, salt, pepper, mustard and vinegar in a clean, warm mixing bowl. (Secure the bowl by wrapping a damp teatowel around its base to keep it steady on the bench. Alternatively, ask somebody to hold the bowl in place.)

With a clean balloon whisk, whisk these ingredients together until light gold in colour. Whisk in the oil, almost drop by drop until you have added a third. Slowly increase the flow of oil to a thin, steady stream until all oil has been incorporated. Keeps, refrigerated, for up to six days.

60g (2oz) **blue vein cheese**,
such as gorgonzola or Milawa blue
2 teaspoons **white wine vinegar**
1 cup (250ml/8fl oz) traditional **vinaigrette**
(see recipe page 139)

blue cheese dressing

Good gorgonzola, slices of ripe pear and a glass of botrytised wine makes a sensational combination. But as well as gracing any table in its natural state, blue cheese also makes an excellent salad dressing.

makes about 1¼ cups (310ml/10fl oz)

in the Ⓚitchen
Place cheese in a bowl and mash to a paste with the vinegar.
When fully combined, stir in the vinaigrette.
Pour into a storage container.

at the Ⓣable
Shake the dressing well before using. It's the perfect dressing for a Cos lettuce and pear salad, among others. Keeps, refrigerated, for about two weeks.

chilli jam

60g (2oz) large **Thai dried chillies**
315g (10oz) **red Thai shallots**, fried
155g (5oz) **garlic**, fried
60g (2oz) **dried prawns**
250g (8oz) **palm sugar**
125g (4oz) **tamarind** pulp

This gutsy condiment will add a real zing to most barbecue dishes. Warn everyone if your version is particularly feisty.

makes about 1kg (2lb)

chef's note:

Always wear gloves when preparing chillies, but if you suffer a chilli burn, use a milk product to take away the heat. For example, for a chilli burn on the lip, apply some yoghurt; if your tongue is burning, rinse your mouth with milk.

in the Ⓚitchen

Roast the chillies briefly in a dry frying pan. Using a mortar and pestle or food processor, blend all ingredients to a smooth paste. Transfer to a saucepan and bring to the boil over medium heat. Reduce heat and simmer, stirring constantly as jam cooks for five minutes.

Spoon into sterilised jars and cover with lids when cool. It will keep, refrigerated, for a long time.

nam jim dressing

A mortar and pestle is traditionally used to make this versatile Thai dressing. It gives a better result than a food processor.

makes about 1 cup (250ml/8fl oz)

3 cloves **garlic**, peeled and crushed
3 **green chillies**, seeded and roughly chopped
3 **coriander roots**, washed and trimmed
2/3 cup (160ml/5fl oz) freshly squeezed **lime juice**
1/4 cup (60ml/2fl oz) **nam pla** (fish sauce)
30g (1oz) **caster sugar**

in the Ⓚitchen

Combine all ingredients and work to a rough paste. Serve immediately.

chef's note:

This dressing goes extremely well with barbecued chicken breasts and quail.

1 teaspoon **mustard powder**, dried

1 hard-boiled **egg**, roughly chopped

½ cup (125ml/4fl oz) freshly squeezed **orange juice**

1 teaspoon finely grated **orange rind**

1 cup (250ml/8fl oz) pouring **cream**

½ teaspoon **salt**

¼ teaspoon **white pepper**

2 tablespoons chopped **chives**

orange and chive dressing

I developed this recipe for use with strongly flavoured lettuce. Another option is acidulated cream, made very simply by adding a little lemon juice to cream and using it as a dressing.

makes about 1¾ cups (440ml/14fl oz)

in the Ⓚitchen

Mash the mustard and egg together. Add orange juice and rind and mix well. Whisk in cream, salt, pepper and chives.

Check and adjust the seasoning—you may like to add more orange juice.

at the Ⓣable

This dressing should be used immediately.

30g (1oz) **garlic** cloves, peeled

1 cup (250ml/8fl oz) **orange juice**

1 cup (250ml/8fl oz) **tomato sauce**

1 cup (250ml/8fl oz) **red wine**

½ cup (125ml/4fl oz) **golden syrup**,
or maple syrup

¼ cup (60ml/2fl oz) **malt vinegar**

60g (2oz) **onion,** chopped

homemade barbecue sauce

A bottle of this zappy sauce makes an excellent small gift.

makes about 4 cups (1L/32fl oz) / high heat / flat plate

at the Ⓑarbecue

Spray the flat plate lightly with oil, and cook garlic
for four minutes, turning constantly to brown it lightly.
Remove from the heat.

in the Ⓚitchen

Purée garlic with remaining ingredients in a food
processor or blender. Pour into a saucepan and simmer
for 15–20 minutes, or until reduced to the consistency
of commercial tomato sauce.

at the Ⓣable

Serve warm. Keeps, refrigerated, for about two weeks.

255g (8oz) **butter**, at room temperature

1 tablespoon freshly squeezed **lemon juice**

1 tablespoon **seeded mustard**

1 tablespoon chopped **parsley**

1 teaspoon freshly ground **black pepper**

lemon and mustard butter

Compound butters like this are used all the time in traditional cooking. You can flavour your butters with tarragon, anchovy, rosemary, and so on. Harden them in the refrigerator, then scoop out and let their marvellous flavour ooze all over barbecued or grilled meat.

makes about 250g (8oz)

in the Kitchen

Put all ingredients in a bowl and mix well using either your hands or a wooden spoon (or use a whisk, if you prefer.) Scrape the mixed butter into a storage container and refrigerate. Alternatively, shape it into a sausage, roll it up in greaseproof paper or plastic wrap and freeze. This way, it's easy to slice off what you want and pop it on your grilled steak. This is what we used to do at catering college, because we used these butters so much.

garlic oil

2 large heads of **garlic**, each about 60g (2oz), unpeeled
2 cups (500ml/16fl oz) extra virgin **olive oil**

Garlic-infused oil is sensational poured over steamed potatoes and a whole range of barbecued vegetables, lifting the flavour and adding excitement.

makes about 2 cups (500ml/16fl oz) / high heat / flat plate

in the Ⓚitchen

Cut garlic heads, crosswise, about a third of the way from the top of each head. Keep the garlic tops for another use.

at the Ⓑarbecue

Spray the flat plate with oil and cook cut garlic heads, cut-side-down, for seven minutes. Remove from the heat and put into an airtight storage container. Cover with oil and leave to sit for two days before use. If you haven't used the oil within six days of preparing it, remove and discard garlic from the oil, return the lid and store oil in a cool, dark place. Keeps for about two weeks.

200g (7oz) **mushroom caps**
1 cup (250ml / 8fl oz) light **olive oil**

mushroom oil

Once you have become addicted to this fragrant oil, as I have, you will use it day in, day out.

makes about 1¼ cups (310ml/10fl oz) / medium heat / flat plate

chef's note:

All manner of oils flavoured with various ingredients, including basil, rosemary, garlic and truffles, are available commercially. These usually have stabilisers added. With oils infused at home I have found it is best to use them quickly.

in the Ⓚitchen

Cut the mushrooms into slices about 5cm (¼in) thick.

at the Ⓑarbecue

Spray the flat plate with oil and cook the mushrooms for five minutes without adding any more oil. The slices will be lightly browned.

Lift mushrooms into an airtight storage jar and return to the kitchen. Pour olive oil onto the mushrooms, stir, replace lid and keep in a cool dark cupboard for two days.

After the two days, strain the oil to remove and discard all mushroom slices. Use the oil within four days of straining.

155g (5oz) **peanut butter** (smooth or crunchy)

1 cup (250ml/8fl oz) **water**

1 clove **garlic**, peeled and crushed

2 teaspoons **palm sugar**

1 **red chilli**, seeded and roughly chopped

¼ cup (60ml/2fl oz) light **soy sauce**

1 tablespoon **lemon juice**

1 tablespoon **fish sauce**

½ cup (125ml/4fl oz) **coconut milk**

peanut sauce

This is a quick version of a satay sauce, but it is really good to keep on hand to liven up any form of barbecued chicken, veal or prawns.

makes about 2½ cups (625ml/20fl oz)

in the Ⓚitchen

Combine peanut butter and water in a saucepan, stirring over moderate heat until well mixed.

 Remove from heat and add remaining ingredients. Return to moderate heat and cook, stirring, for five to six minutes, or until a thick paste forms. Keeps, refrigerated, for about three weeks.

3 **red capsicum** (bell pepper)

1 large **onion**, peeled and chopped

2 large cloves **garlic**, peeled and crushed

½ cup (125 ml/4 fl oz) **white wine**

½ cup (125 ml/4 fl oz) **cider vinegar**

3 cups (750 ml/24 fl oz) **olive oil**

2 tablespoons roughly chopped fresh **thyme** leaves

¼ teaspoon **salt**

cayenne pepper, optional

red capsicum sauce

The same ingredient can have different names in various parts of the world. In the United States, fresh coriander is called cilantro and a capsicum is called a bell pepper or a pepper, depending on where you are.

makes about 5 cups (1.25L/40fl oz)

in the Ⓚitchen

Remove the seeds and cores from the capsicum and chop the flesh finely.
Place in saucepan with remaining ingredients, except cayenne pepper.
Bring to the boil and simmer for one-and-a-quarter hours.

   Purée in a food processor or blender and strain. Taste and adjust seasoning, adding a little cayenne pepper if you like. Pour into sterilised jars and cool.
Keeps, refrigerated, for two weeks.

¼ cup (60ml/2 fl oz) **olive oil**, or vegetable oil

1 clove **garlic**, peeled and crushed

½ teaspoon **dry Dijon mustard**

1 tablespoon **wine vinegar**

1 tablespoon finely chopped **parsley**

½ teaspoon **salt**

¼ teaspoon **white pepper**

traditional vinaigrette

This simple dressing has featured on dining tables all over the world. It has a big flavour impact when combined with salad vegetables.

makes about ⅓ cup (80ml/2½ fl oz)

in the Ⓚitchen

For the very best results, this dressing must be made by hand. Put the oil, garlic and mustard in a large bowl and whisk with a balloon whisk until the mixture is a creamy consistency and light yellow in colour. Whisking aerates and blends extremely well.

Whisk in the vinegar and add parsley, salt and pepper. Stir until combined.

at the Ⓣable

The best way to coat salad leaves with vinaigrette is to tumble them in a small amount of dressing. There should never be any dressing left sitting in the bottom of the bowl.

Alternatively, serve the dressing separately and have guests help themselves. This way any leftover salad can be refrigerated and used at another meal.

variations on the vinaigrette theme

- Crumble two hard-boiled egg yolks into the dressing at the last minute. Dice the egg whites and add to the salad ingredients.
- Add 2 teaspoons each of finely chopped capers, gherkins and green olive flesh to the mixture at the last minute.
- Substitute 2 tablespoons of orange juice for the 1 tablespoon of vinegar if you like a citrus flavour.

glossary

bocconcini small balls of fresh mozzarella, preserved in whey and with a moist, springy texture.

bok choy (Chinese chard) chinese cabbage-like vegetable with white, fleshy stems and green leaves.

brioche sweet yeast bread made with eggs and butter.

candlenut creamy-coloured, round hard nut, similar to the macadamia.

celeriac white, tuberous root with a mild celery-like flavour.

coriander (cilantro) root root of the coriander plant, of which the leaves are widely used.

'cheeks' lemon, lime or capsicum cheeks are the sides of the fruits cut around the core so the seeds are eliminated.

Desiree potato oval potato with smooth, pink skin and yellow flesh.

demiglace concentrated beef-based sauce.

eschalot small onion bulb, sweet and mild in flavour, with thin reddish-brown skin.

garam masala spice mixture, usually consisting of cumin, cloves, cardamom, nutmeg and pepper.

gorgonzola soft, creamy-white cow's milk cheese with greenish-blue veins.

green onions (scallion) young immature onion, with slender white bulb and green tube-like leaves. Spring onions are similar, but younger with a smaller bulb.

Kipfler potato elongated potato with pale yellow skin and waxy flesh.

lemon myrtle green leaf with lemon, lemon grass and lime oil flavours, obtained from an Australian native rainforest tree.

lemon pepper cracked lemon-flavoured peppercorns.

Lebanese cucumber short, narrow cucumber with smooth skin.

mascarpone soft, smooth creamy cheese, made from pure cow's cream and high in fat.

mirin sweetened Japanese rice wine with low alcohol content.

palm sugar hard, dense sugar made from palm sap. Varies from creamy-white to dark brown in colour.

pancetta unsmoked cured bacon from the belly of the pig.

pepperberries native Australian berries, larger than regular peppercorns and with a stronger taste.

pink peppercorns unripe berries from the pepper tree.

Pontiac potato round potato with red skin and white, waxy flesh.

raw sugar large crystals of sugar, golden in colour and made from clarified cane juice.

Sichuan peppercorns berries from the prickly ash (unrelated to the peppercorn) with an intense flavour.

semi-roasted tomatoes tomatoes (usually Roma) which have been roasted for a long period at a very low temperature until they are semi-dried.

sweetlip species of the reef fish known as emperor, with white, moist and flaky flesh.

tahini smooth paste of ground sesame seeds.

telegraph cucumber long, thin almost seedless cucumber with dark green skin.

Vietnamese mint strong-tasting, aromatic green leaf, also known as Cambodian mint. Not a true mint.

index

q–r

s

t

v–z

First published in Australia in 2000 by

New Holland Publishers (Australia) Pty Ltd

Canadian Cataloguing in Publication Data available upon request

ISBN 1-55263-199-0

The Canada Council | Le Conseil des Arts
FOR THE ARTS | du Canada
SINCE 1957 | DEPUIS 1957

The publisher gratefully acknowledges the support of the Canada Council for the Arts and
the Ontario Arts Council for its publishing program.

We acknowledge the financial support of the Government of Canada through the Book
Publishing Industry Development Program (BPIDP) for our publishing activities.

Key Porter Books Limited

70 The Esplanade

Toronto, Ontario

Canada M5E 1R2

www.keyporter.com

Publishing General Manager: Jane Hazell

Publisher: Averill Chase

Project Editor: Sophie Church

Copy Editor: Lynn Cole

Design and illustration: Peta Nugent

Photographer: Joe Filshie

Food Stylist: Georgie Dolling

Home Economist: Christine Shepperd

Reproduction: Colour Gallery, Malaysia

Printed and bound in Canada

This book is typeset in News Gothic.

Accessories provided by Boda Nova, Dinosaur Designs,
General Electric Outdoor Kitchen Centre, Lincraft, Parterre Encore,
Studio Ramsay, Witchery.